Reading FORWARD

BASIC 1

Reading FORWARD

BASIC 1

Series Editors Bin-na Yang, Dong-sook Kim

Project Editors Jung-ah Lee, Mina Song, Mi-youn Woo, Jee-young Song, Kyung-hee Kim, Na-hyun Ahn, Eun-kyung Kim

Contributing Writers Patrick Ferraro, Henry John Amen IV, John Boswell, Robert Vernon, Keeran Murphy, Peter Morton

Illustrators Seol-hee Kim, Hyun-il Bang, Hyun-jin Choi, Hyo-sil Lee

Design Ho-hyun Bang, Hyun-jung Jang, Yeon-joo Kim

Editorial Designer In-sun Lee

ISBN 979-11-253-0796-9 53740

INTRODUCTION

★
★
★
Reading Forward is a six-level series of three progressive steps: Basic, Intermediate, and Advanced. Based on the essential needs of young students, the series focuses on a specific goal: expanding vocabulary and knowledge. This goal guides all of the content and activities in the series. The first step of the series will enlarge vocabulary, and the later steps will increase knowledge. Thus, the series will eventually help students improve their reading comprehension.

Each book of Reading Forward is composed of 20 units. The number of words used in each reading passage is as follows.

Step 3
Reading Forward
Advanced
for Knowledge
1 : 240 – 260 words
2 : 260 – 280 words

Step 2
Reading Forward
Intermediate
for Vocabulary & Knowledge
1 : 200 – 220 words
2 : 220 – 240 words

Step 1
Reading Forward
Basic
for Vocabulary
1 : 150 – 170 words
2 : 170 – 190 words

Key Features of Reading Forward Series

– Current, high-interest topics are developed in an easy way so that students can understand them. These subjects can hold their attention and keep them motivated to read forward.

– Comprehension checkup questions presented in the series are based on standardized test questions. These can help students prepare for English tests at school, as well as official English language tests.

– Each unit is designed to enlarge vocabulary by presenting intensive activities for learning vocabulary at both the beginning and the end of each unit. Students can learn the key words in each passage and effectively improve their vocabulary.

FORMAT

Vocabulary Preview
Before reading each passage, students can preview the key words through two activities: definition – word matching and finding synonyms or antonyms.

Before Reading
The question before each passage allows students to think about the topic by relating it to their lives. It also helps students become interested in the passage before reading it.

Reading
This part serves as the main passage of the unit, and it explains an intriguing and instructive topic in great depth. As students progress through the book, the content of these passages becomes more and more substantial.

Reading Comprehension
The reading is followed by different types of questions, which test understanding of the passage. The various types of questions focus on important reading skills, such as understanding the main idea and organization of the passage, identifying details, and drawing inferences.

Strategic Summary / Organizer
Each unit includes a strategic summary or organizer of the main reading passage. It gives students a better understanding of the important points and organization of the passage. These exercises focus on further development of effective reading comprehension skills.

Vocabulary Review
A review of the key vocabulary concludes each unit. Three types of exercises test understanding of new words: matching definitions, identifying synonyms and antonyms, and completing sentences with the correct words in context.

Word Book
A list of the key words from each unit is presented in a handy book for convenience. It provides students with an easy reference to new vocabulary.

MP3 Files
Audio recordings of all reading passages are available to be downloaded for free at www.nebooks.co.kr.

TABLE OF CONTENTS

Reading Forward

★ ★ ★

Unit ★ 01

PLACES

A Connect each word to its correct definition.

1 the people who work for a company   •   • *a.* staff

2 to travel through a place to learn about it   •   • *b.* grain

3 a seed from a crop like rice, wheat, or corn   •   • *c.* harvest

4 the time when crops are gathered from the fields •   • *d.* explore

B Write the word that has the opposite meaning of each word.

enter	giant	reach	amusing

1 tiny : _____

2 exit : _____

3 boring : _____

4 depart : _____

★ The Corn Maze

I'm Andy. Today I went to the corn *maze in Dixon, California. (①) It's the largest corn maze in the world. (②) I was really
5 surprised at its size. (③) It's over 200,000 m²! (④) It was amusing to see a lot of people waiting in line to enter.

Up close, the maze just
10 looked like a field of tall corn plants. However, I could see the design of the maze from a higher place. This year it is designed to look like a giant pumpkin. I heard that it looked like the Statue of Liberty last year.

In the maze, I didn't know where to go, even with a map. The corn was so tall that I couldn't see anything around me. I almost got lost! After two
15 hours, I finally reached the end with help from the staff.

After exploring the maze, I took a corn bath, which was filled with corn grains. It felt strange but nice! I recommend that you visit the maze, too.

*maze: a group of connected paths that
is difficult to find your way through

READING COMPREHENSION

1 What is the passage mainly about?

a. Joining a corn harvest

b. A visit to an animal farm

c. A trip to a maze in a corn field

d. An exciting adventure in a jungle

2 Where would the following sentence best fit?

> The maze is a popular tourist spot during the harvest season in fall.

a. ①   b. ②   c. ③   d. ④

3 Which is NOT mentioned about the corn maze?

a. its location
b. its opening hours
c. its size
d. its design

4 Why wasn't Andy able to find the way out even with a map?

Because _____ .

5 What can be inferred from the passage?

a. The maze is built for children only.
b. The design of the maze changes every year.
c. You have to pay an entrance fee to take a corn bath.
d. You can win a prize when you reach the end of the maze.

STRATEGIC SUMMARY

Fill in the blanks with the correct words.

Andy visited the largest _____ maze in the world. It's located in Dixon, California. He was very surprised at the _____ of it — over 200,000 m². From above, it was designed to look like a giant _____. It took him two hours to find his way out. In the end, he needed help from the staff. Afterwards, he took a corn _____. It felt nice. And he recommends the experience.

| size | bath | corn | tourist | pumpkin |

VOCABULARY REVIEW

A Complete the sentences with the words in the box. (Change the form if needed.)

season	pumpkin	bath	map	recommend

1 I always use a _____ when I go to a new place.

2 I'm covered in sweat. I want to take a _____ now.

3 This book is really interesting. I _____ that you read it.

4 The climate is very hot and humid during the rainy _____.

B Find the word that has a similar meaning to the underlined word.

1 The Louvre Museum is full of <u>tourists</u> from all around the world.

    a. artists   *b.* singers   *c.* travelers   *d.* designers

2 This magazine introduces many amazing holiday <u>spots</u> for families.

    a. plans   *b.* places   *c.* presents   *d.* traditions

C Choose the best word to complete each sentence.

1 The roads are _____ to form a crisscross pattern.

    a. grown   *b.* dropped   *c.* touched   *d.* designed

2 A farmer is driving a tractor across the wheat _____.

    a. field   *b.* flour   *c.* forest   *d.* product

3 How many countries did you _____ on your trip to Europe?

    a. walk   *b.* visit   *c.* break   *d.* follow

4 These potted _____ need to be watered once a month.

    a. fish   *b.* fields   *c.* plants   *d.* animals

HEALTH

A Connect each word to its correct definition.

1 smelling very unpleasant • • *a.* active

2 feeling uncomfortable and ashamed • • *b.* stinky

3 having a lot of energy and doing many activities • • *c.* sweat

4 liquid that appears on your skin when you are hot • • *d.* embarrassed

B Write the word that has the opposite meaning of each word.

dry same cause reduce

1 wet : _____

2 prevent : _____

3 increase : _____

4 different : _____

★ *Foot Odor*

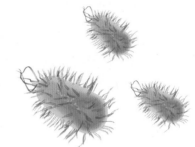

Q: I'm embarrassed because my feet are stinky. What causes the bad smell? How can I get rid of it? I need some help.

A: Hello, I'm Dr. Page. I think I can help you with
5   your problem. ① The bad smell is caused by tiny bacteria on your feet. ② They eat the sweat on your feet and then produce waste. ③ People usually sweat about 500 ml a day. ④ This waste makes your feet very stinky. When your feet sweat a lot, it gets worse because the bacteria become very active!

To get rid of the smell, you should wash your feet often. This will wash away the sweat. You should also dry your feet well, especially between your toes. This is because _____(A)_____. Wearing socks made of cotton helps your feet stay dry. And you need to keep your shoes dry and try not to wear the same shoes every day. Finally, soak your feet in warm water mixed with a little vinegar for 15 minutes. The vinegar kills bacteria and reduces the smell.

READING COMPREHENSION

1 **What is Dr. Page mainly talking about?**

   a. How to avoid foot disease

   b. The bad smells of our bodies

   c. What makes you sweat so much

   d. The causes of and solutions for smelly feet

2 Which sentence is NOT needed in the passage?

    a. ①   *b.* ②   *c.* ③   *d.* ④

3 Why do stinky feet smell worse when your feet sweat a lot?

Because _____ .

4 What is the best choice for blank (A)?

    a. bacteria love damp places
    b. it helps bacteria become inactive
    c. it causes bacteria to get rid of waste
    d. bacteria don't like the sweat on your feet

5 What is NOT mentioned as a way to reduce foot odor?

    a. Wash one's feet as often as possible.
    b. Keep one's feet warm and wet.
    c. Wear different shoes every day.
    d. Use vinegar to kill bacteria on one's feet.

STRATEGIC ORGANIZER

Fill in the blanks with the correct words.

Foot Odor

What makes feet smell bad
- Bacteria on your feet eat _____ .
- The _____ they produce smells bad.

How to _____ the smell
- Wash your feet often and dry your feet well.
- Wear dry shoes and _____ them every day.
- Soak your feet in warm water with some _____ .

| waste | sweat | change | vinegar | get rid of |

★ ★ ★
VOCABULARY REVIEW

A Write the correct word next to its definition.

| toe | soak | stay | waste | vinegar |

1 useless leftover matter: _____

2 to put something in a liquid for a while: _____

3 a sour liquid that is used to add flavor to food: _____

4 one of the five small parts at the end of a foot: _____

B Find the word that has a similar meaning to the underlined word.

1 This factory has been <u>producing</u> digital cameras.

    a. buying   *b.* avoiding   *c.* providing   *d.* creating

2 Can you <u>get rid of</u> these stains on this dress?

    a. watch   *b.* remove   *c.* increase   *d.* recommend

C Choose the best word to complete each sentence.

1 If you don't clean your kitchen, _____ will grow there.

    a. nails   *b.* height   *c.* flowers   *d.* bacteria

2 If you can't carry those boxes, ask for his _____.

    a. help   *b.* smell   *c.* worry   *d.* problem

3 Add butter and eggs to flour and _____ them in a bowl.

    a. eat   *b.* mix   *c.* crush   *d.* wash

4 My shoes got _____ after I walked in the rain.

    a. dry   *b.* tight   *c.* damp   *d.* colorful

LITERATURE

A Connect each word to its correct definition.

1 a jar used to hold flowers • • *a.* steal

2 food that you eat between meals • • *b.* vase

3 to take something that isn't yours • • *c.* snack

4 an area in which flowers and plants are grown • • *d.* garden

B Write the word that has the opposite meaning of each word.

accept	scold	stay	wrong

1 leave : _____   *2* right : _____

3 reject : _____   *4* praise : _____

★ *My Sweet Orange Tree*

One day, the teacher asks Zeze to stay after class. She scolds him because he stole some flowers from someone's garden and gave them to her.

Teacher : Zeze, why did you steal these flowers? Don't you know stealing is wrong?

5 **Zeze** : I wanted to give you flowers. But I don't have any money or a garden.

Teacher : But why?

Zeze : So you could put them in the empty vase on your desk. You always do nice

10 things for me, like giving me money for snacks.

Teacher : I can give you snack money every day if you need it.

Zeze : I can't accept it every day. There are

15 other students who are poorer than me, like Dorotilia. She has ten brothers and sisters, and her mother has to do laundry to earn money. My mother taught me to always share with poorer people.

Teacher : *(putting a hand on Zeze's shoulder)* I understand. But please don't bring me any more flowers unless someone gives them to you. Okay?

Zeze : Okay, I promise. But will your vase always be empty?

Teacher : No, it will never be empty. When I look at it, I'll always see the most beautiful flowers in the world. And I'll think that my best student gave them to me.

READING COMPREHENSION

1 **What is the story mainly about?**

   a. Zeze's first day at school

   b. Zeze's bad habit of stealing

   c. Zeze's flowers for his teacher

   d. Zeze and Dorotilia's friendship

2 What did Zeze want the teacher to do with the flowers?

_____

3 Why can't Zeze take money from the teacher every day?

    a. He is too shy to take the money from her.

    b. He doesn't need it because he has some money.

    c. He worries about the poorer students in his class.

    d. He doesn't want the other students to know that he is poor.

4 Based on the story, what does the phrase <u>the most beautiful flowers</u> suggest?

    a. an expensive gift for Zeze

    b. Zeze's love for the teacher

    c. the flowers that Zeze stole

    d. the teacher's poor students

5 What is the best word to describe Zeze?

    a. brave   *b.* playful

    c. cheerful   *d.* warm-hearted

STRATEGIC SUMMARY

Fill in the blanks with the correct words.

Zeze steals some _____ and gives them to his teacher. She scolds him and tells him that stealing is _____. He explains that he wanted to _____ her for doing kind things for him; therefore he wanted to give her something to put in the empty vase on her desk. The teacher says that the vase on her desk will never be _____ again. And she also says she will always see beautiful flowers from her best student in it.

> empty   wrong   thank   garden   flowers

VOCABULARY REVIEW

A Complete the sentences with the words in the box. (Change the form if needed.)

laundry	bring	unless	promise	always

1 Can I use your pen? I forgot to _____ mine.

2 He _____ to come back soon, but he never returned.

3 If you don't have clean clothes, you'd better do _____.

4 Don't leave the classroom _____ your teacher says it's okay.

B Find the word that has the opposite meaning of the underlined word.

1 The restaurant was <u>empty</u> when they went there for dinner.

    a. open   *b.* loud   *c.* closed   *d.* full

2 They could not buy new shoes because they were <u>poor</u>.

    a. short   *b.* rich   *c.* stupid   *d.* tired

C Choose the best word to complete each sentence.

1 I _____ a room with my sister because our apartment is small.

    a. put   *b.* take   *c.* share   *d.* waste

2 If you spend more than you _____, you will use up all your savings.

    a. earn   *b.* count   *c.* send   *d.* throw

3 To become good friends, you should try to _____ each other better.

    a. hurt   *b.* steal   *c.* leave   *d.* understand

4 The girl looked very cold, so I covered her _____ with a blanket.

    a. scarf   *b.* eyes   *c.* shoulders   *d.* vase

Unit ★ 04

PSYCHOLOGY

A Connect each word to its correct definition.

1 the ability to do what you want •   • *a.* sale

2 a person who buys goods or services •   • *b.* theory

3 an idea that shows how and why something happens •   • *c.* freedom

4 an event in which a shop sells its goods at lower prices • • *d.* customer

B Write the word that has the opposite meaning of each word.

> silent   allow   recover   turn off

1 lose : _____

2 noisy : _____

3 prohibit : _____

4 switch on : _____

★ The Reactance Theory

Imagine that your teacher tells you to turn off your smartphone during class. What do you want to do? You want to use it more! Why is that? The reactance theory explains the

5 reason.

It says that people have the freedom to decide what to do. When someone tells you to do something, you feel you're losing your freedom.

10 So, you feel like doing the opposite to recover your lost freedom. Moreover, your feeling becomes greater when your freedom is more strongly restricted. Think about how deeply Romeo and Juliet loved each other when they weren't

15 allowed to!

Many companies use this theory to _____(A)_____. For example, they often use expressions like "limited edition" or "one-day-only sale." They limit customers' freedom to buy their products any time they want. Then the customers feel they need to buy the products before the sale

20 is over.

So, if you need your brother to keep silent for a while, don't yell "Be quiet!"

READING COMPREHENSION

1 What is the best title for the passage?

a. Go Fight for Your Freedom!

b. Who Created the Reactance Theory?

c. How to Attract Customers during a Sale

d. The Background and Use of the Reactance Theory

2 Why does the writer mention the underlined part?

    a. To describe the writer's experience

    b. To give a real-life example of a theory

    c. To show how to prove a scientific theory

    d. To explain the bad points of using a smartphone

3 What happens when our freedom is lost by someone telling us what to do?

_____

4 What is the best choice for blank (A)?

    a. advertise their products cheaply

    b. show respect to their customers

    c. make people want their products more

    d. get more information about their customers

5 Who is NOT talking about the reactance theory?

    a. Chris: I want to buy the new book because it is a limited edition.

    b. Nick: I pressed the button even though I saw the "Do Not Press" sign.

    c. Kay: All of my friends bought smartphones, so I decided to buy one, too.

    d. Jessica: When my mom tells me to study hard, I want to go out and play.

STRATEGIC SUMMARY

Fill in the blanks with the correct words.

We don't like to lose our freedom to _____ what to do. When we're told what to do, we think our freedom is _____. So we do the opposite to _____ our freedom. This is called the reactance theory. It is often used by companies. By _____ the freedom to buy their products, the companies make customers feel they should buy the products.

| lost | decide | limiting | recover | sell |

VOCABULARY REVIEW

A Write the correct word next to its definition.

lose	limit	product	decide	expression

1 to not have something anymore: _____

2 to make a choice about something: _____

3 something made in a factory to be sold: _____

4 a group of words with a special meaning: _____

B Find the word that has a similar meaning to the underlined word.

1 Can you <u>explain</u> the rules of baseball to me?

   a. allow   *b.* expect   *c.* discuss   *d.* describe

2 The meeting <u>was over</u> about half an hour ago.

   a. started   *b.* finished   *c.* took place   *d.* was canceled

C Choose the best word to complete each sentence.

1 The word "light" means the _____ of the word "heavy."

   a. front   *b.* top   *c.* opposite   *d.* same

2 Speed is _____ to 30 kilometers per hour in the school zone.

   a. gained   *b.* accessed   *c.* provided   *d.* restricted

3 David tried to _____ the scene, but nothing came to mind.

   a. use   *b.* forget   *c.* become   *d.* imagine

4 The teacher wanted to know the _____ why I was so late.

   a. plan   *b.* period   *c.* reason   *d.* reactance

Unit ★ 05
ART

A Connect each word to its correct definition.

1 funny and light-hearted •   • **a.** appeal

2 a specialized way of doing an activity •   • **b.** playful

3 a person who appears in a film or story •   • **c.** technique

4 to be interesting or attractive to someone •   • **d.** character

B Write the word that has the opposite meaning of each word.

silly   comedy   male   suddenly

1 slowly : _____   2 serious : _____

3 female : _____   4 tragedy : _____

★ *The Trocks*

At a ballet, the dancers come onto the stage wearing lovely dresses and make-up. But there is something strange about this ballet. The dancers are all
5 men! It is a performance of Les Ballets Trockadero de Monte Carlo (the Trocks), a world-famous men's ballet group.

The Trocks ballet group was started in 1974 in New York and is well known
10 for its _____ (A) _____.
Male dancers play all the female parts. Imagine big men wearing ballet skirts and dancing on their toes. It is very amusing! (①) In addition, they change serious classical
15 ballet stories into comedies. (②) In their version, however, the swan dies suddenly, like a cartoon character. (③) What's more, the dancers make some mistakes to make their performance funnier. (④) For instance, they sometimes fall off the stage so that the audience can laugh.
20 Besides the humor, the Trocks group is famous for its well-trained ballet dancers. They show excellent ballet technique while they act silly. So the performances appeal to both fans of ballet and fans of comedy at the same time.

READING COMPREHENSION

1 What is the passage mainly about?

a. What makes a ballet group popular

b. Why a special ballet group was started

c. What roles male ballet dancers play on stage

d. How male dancers are different from female ones

2 What is the best choice for blank (A)?

a. beautiful performers

b. interesting costumes

c. difficult dance moves

d. playful performances

3 Where would the following sentence best fit?

> For example, in *The Dying Swan*, the swan should die gracefully.

a. ①   b. ②   c. ③   d. ④

4 Why do Trocks performances appeal to both fans of ballet and fans of comedy?

Because _____ .

5 What is NOT mentioned about the Trocks?

a. When the group first began performing

b. What the dancers do on stage to be funny

c. How the dancers make the audience join in performances

d. How skillful the dancers are

STRATEGIC ORGANIZER

Fill in the blanks with the correct words.

The Trocks

Comical side

• _____ dancers dress and dance like female dancers.

• Classical ballet stories are changed into comedies.

• Dancers make mistakes to make their performance _____ .

_____ quality of dancing

• Dancers are well trained.

• Dancers show excellent ballet _____ .

| high | male | lovely | funnier | technique |

VOCABULARY REVIEW

A Complete the sentences with the words in the box. (Change the form if needed.)

| fan | humor | version | audience | performance |

1 I got a ticket for a live _____ by my favorite band.

2 He is a famous comedian. He has a good sense of _____.

3 Amy is a big _____ of the actor. She has seen all his movies.

4 When the singer finished singing, the _____ began clapping.

B Find the word that has a similar meaning to the underlined word.

1 This restaurant is well known for its seafood pasta.

    a. poor   *b.* famous   *c.* delicious   *d.* expensive

2 The actress stepped onto the stage gracefully.

    a. quickly   *b.* suddenly   *c.* slowly   *d.* beautifully

C Choose the best word to complete each sentence.

1 He likes to tell jokes and make people _____.

    a. lie   *b.* cry   *c.* laugh   *d.* forget

2 In the musical, he's going to _____ a leading part.

    a. play   *b.* deal   *c.* ask   *d.* charge

3 The actor always goes over his lines before going on _____.

    a. game   *b.* yard   *c.* stage   *d.* court

4 My mom is a(n) _____ cook. The dishes she makes are really good.

    a. cheap   *b.* funny   *c.* terrible   *d.* excellent

Unit ★ 06

SPORTS

A Connect each word to its correct definition.

1 difficult to do • • **a.** race

2 going up a slope or a hill • • **b.** local

3 relating to a particular area or city • • **c.** uphill

4 a competition to decide who is the fastest • • **d.** challenging

B Write the word that has the opposite meaning of each word.

miss	meet	strict	steep

1 loose : _____ 2 gradual : _____

3 achieve : _____ 4 not satisfy : _____

★ *The Boston Marathon*

In Boston, the third Monday in April is Patriots' Day. The day is also called "Marathon Monday."

5   The Boston Marathon started as a local event in 1897 with just 18 runners. Now, it's the world's oldest and largest

10   annual marathon. Every year, about 30,000 runners from all around the world run in the race.

The race is not only popular but also very challenging for the runners. (①) Usually, marathons are open to everyone. (②) For example, a

15   20-year-old male runner must hold a marathon record of 3:05:00 or less. (③) The standards are so strict that the runners can miss qualifying by just a second. (④) Also, the Boston Marathon has an uphill road called Heartbreak Hill on its course. Although this hill is not particularly steep or long, it is a big challenge for the runners. That's because it comes after they are almost out

20   of energy.

_____(A)_____ its challenging nature, the Boston Marathon is loved by many people. Crowds of 500,000 cheer at this event. Why not watch and enjoy the Boston Marathon for yourself?

READING COMPREHENSION

1 What is the best title for the passage?

a. How to Train for Your First Marathon

b. What Makes the Boston Marathon Special

c. Patriots' Day: A Special Holiday for Boston

d. The Boston Marathon: A New Sports Event for Everyone

2 Where would the following sentence best fit?

> But in the Boston Marathon, runners have to meet the standards of time limit.

a. ①   *b.* ②   *c.* ③   *d.* ④

3 Why is Heartbreak Hill especially difficult for the runners of the Boston Marathon?

Because _____.

4 What is the best choice for blank (A)?

a. In case of   *b.* Instead of
c. In spite of   *d.* In addition to

5 What is NOT mentioned about the Boston Marathon?

a. Who started it
b. When it was first held
c. How often it is held
d. How runners qualify for it

STRATEGIC ORGANIZER

Fill in the blanks with the correct words.

The Boston Marathon

- It was first held in 1897, when only 18 runners _____ in it.
- Now, it is a(n) _____ race, and about 30,000 runners participate in it every year.

Its challenging features
- It has _____ time standards that runners must meet.
- Runners have to run Heartbreak Hill after they are almost out of _____.

| energy | local | strict | took part | international |

VOCABULARY REVIEW

A Write the correct word next to its definition.

hill	annual	patriot	course	crowd

1 happening every year: _____

2 a person who loves his or her country: _____

3 a large group of people gathered together: _____

4 an area of land or water where a sports event takes place: _____

B Find the word that has a similar meaning to the underlined word.

1 He <u>held</u> the world record in the long jump in 2010.

    a. set   *b.* had   *c.* wrote   *d.* challenged

2 That TV program is not good for children because of its violent <u>nature</u>.

    a. changes   *b.* characteristics   *c.* language   *d.* environment

C Choose the best word to complete each sentence.

1 Driving faster than the speed _____ is illegal.

    a. number   *b.* limit   *c.* amount   *d.* control

2 Usain Bolt broke the world _____ in the 100-meter sprint.

    a. race   *b.* peace   *c.* record   *d.* power

3 We don't sell the product if it doesn't meet our safety _____.

    a. signs   *b.* devices   *c.* standards   *d.* education

4 He felt encouraged when his family _____ for him.

    a. cheered   *b.* asked   *c.* waited   *d.* prepared

Unit ★ 07

MEDIA

A Connect each word to its correct definition.

1 to remove something • • *a.* delete

2 suddenly and surprisingly • • *b.* tradition

3 a very old custom, belief, or story • • *c.* information

4 knowledge about someone or something • • *d.* unexpectedly

B Write the word that has the opposite meaning of each word.

reward	secretly	show up	simple

1 complex : _____

2 publicly : _____

3 disappear : _____

4 punishment : _____

★ *Easter Eggs*

One day, when you are searching for information on the Internet, you type a certain word and click "search." Then, a small computer game shows up on your browser. This is not an error. This is an "*Easter egg."

5   An Easter egg is a bit of hidden content in a computer program, such as a simple message, image, or game. Easter eggs can be found unexpectedly by pressing certain keys at once or clicking the mouse a certain way. The name "Easter egg" comes from the Easter tradition of

10 hiding eggs for children to find. (①) Similarly, programmers secretly put Easter eggs in their products. (②) However, this kind of Easter egg isn't only found in computer programs. (③) For example, you can find deleted scenes or interviews with the actors. (④)

    So why do programmers make and hide Easter eggs? They do

15 so because people love to find a surprise. <u>Some people check the menu in a DVD or a computer program just to find this hidden reward!</u>

*Easter: a Christian holiday celebrated in the spring

READING COMPREHENSION

1 **What is the passage mainly about?**

   a. A playful game of hide-and-seek

   b. Hidden surprises called Easter eggs

   c. Why people love behind-the-scenes stories

   d. Serious errors found in computer programs

2 How does the writer introduce the topic?

    a. By explaining the origin of Easter eggs

    b. By introducing some famous Easter eggs

    c. By mentioning various kinds of Easter eggs

    d. By describing how an Easter egg might be found

3 How can we unexpectedly find an Easter egg?

_____

4 Where would the following sentence best fit?

There are many hidden features in DVDs, too.

    a. ①   *b.* ②   *c.* ③   *d.* ④

5 What can be inferred from the underlined sentence?

    a. This kind of hidden content interests people.

    b. People are annoyed at the unnecessary content.

    c. Some people want to make their own Easter eggs.

    d. Hiding an Easter egg will not be allowed in the future.

STRATEGIC SUMMARY

Fill in the blanks with the correct words.

An "Easter egg" is a bit of _____ content in a computer program. This name comes from the tradition of hiding eggs for children on Easter. It can be a simple message or game. You can find an Easter egg by _____ keys or clicking the mouse. This kind of content can also be found in some DVDs in the form of deleted _____ or interviews. Easter eggs are created because people enjoy _____ surprising things.

finding   browser   hidden   pressing   scenes

VOCABULARY REVIEW

A Complete the sentences with the words in the box. (Change the form if needed.)

scene	browser	press	hide	error

1 The closing _____ of the movie was very sad.

2 He _____ the button, but nothing happened.

3 Her parents decided to _____ her present until her birthday.

4 There are so many _____ in this computer game that I can't play it.

B Find the word that has a similar meaning to the underlined word.

1 The police searched for the missing child.

    a. looked after   *b.* waited for   *c.* looked for   *d.* found out

2 The giant panda eats only a certain type of bamboo.

    a. soft   *b.* particular   *c.* delicious   *d.* common

C Choose the best word to complete each sentence.

1 Don't just memorize the whole book. You need to understand its _____.

    a. bookmark   *b.* letters   *c.* contents   *d.* condition

2 If you call me and I'm out, please leave a _____ with the front desk.

    a. mark   *b.* spot   *c.* tip   *d.* message

3 You can't do more than one job _____.

    a. at least   *b.* at once   *c.* by chance   *d.* out of the blue

4 If you want to capture the image, select COPY from the main _____.

    a. gate   *b.* side   *c.* idea   *d.* menu

Unit ★ 08

ORIGINS

A Connect each word to its correct definition.

1 to copy someone or something •
2 a place where you can buy and eat a meal •
3 to cook something with dry heat in an oven •
4 the boxes, bottles, etc. used for wrapping products •

• **a.** bake
• **b.** follow
• **c.** restaurant
• **d.** packaging

B Write the word that has the opposite meaning of each word.

| regular | famous | melt | tiny |

1 huge : _____   2 freeze : _____

3 unusual : _____   4 unknown : _____

★ *Chocolate Chip Cookies*

Before Reading
What is your favorite kind of cookie?

Everyone loves chocolate chip cookies. These popular cookies were created by a woman named Ruth Wakefield in Boston in 1933.

One day, Ruth was baking cookies for her
5   restaurant, the Toll House Inn. Because she ran out of melting chocolate, she used regular chocolate instead. ① She cut it into tiny pieces expecting them to melt in the oven. ② Cookies are usually baked for 10 to 15 minutes. ③ To Ruth's surprise, the chocolate didn't melt. ④ The result was a sweet and delicious cookie with softened chocolate chips! People
10 loved it so much that her recipe was even printed in a Boston newspaper.

Meanwhile, Nestle, a food company, realized that sales of its chocolate increased greatly in Boston. That's because Ruth used the company's chocolate to make the cookies, and many people followed her recipe. So Nestle bought the recipe and printed it on its chocolate packaging. Soon, chocolate chip cookies became famous across the country. Today, chocolate chip cookies are still sometimes called Toll House cookies in America.

READING COMPREHENSION

1 **What is the best title for the passage?**

   a. The First Chocolate Chip Cookies
   b. How to Make Chocolate Chip Cookies
   c. What Makes People Love Chocolate Chip Cookies?
   d. Chocolate Chip Cookies: A Popular Snack for Children

2 Which sentence is NOT needed in the passage?

    a. ①   *b.* ②   *c.* ③   *d.* ④

3 What can be inferred from the 2nd paragraph?

    a. Ruth's cookies tasted bad.

    b. Ruth ran a famous restaurant.

    c. Chocolate chip cookies were made by chance.

    d. Newspapers offered free cookies to their readers.

4 Why did the sales of Nestle's chocolate increase in Boston?

Because _____ .

5 What is NOT mentioned about chocolate chip cookies?

    a. Who created them

    b. When they were created

    c. How people reacted to them

    d. How they became famous around the world

STRATEGIC SUMMARY

Fill in the blanks with the correct words.

Chocolate chip cookies were invented in 1933 by Ruth Wakefield. She owned a _____ in Boston called the Toll House Inn. One day, she put regular chocolate in her cookies instead of _____ chocolate. It didn't melt, and the result was the first chocolate chip cookies. People loved them and followed Ruth's _____ . A food company printed it on its chocolate packaging, and soon the cookies became _____ all across America.

| recipe | tiny | melting | restaurant | popular |

★ ★ ★
VOCABULARY REVIEW

A Complete the sentences with the words in the box. (Change the form if needed.)

print	sale	recipe	surprise	soften

1 This cream will _____ the skin on your hands.

2 If you follow this _____, you can make a delicious pizza.

3 The number of calories in each product is _____ on its label.

4 To our _____, all passengers on board survived the plane crash.

B Find the word that has a similar meaning to the underlined word.

1 They <u>ran out of</u> the gas for the heater.

    a. replaced   *b.* bought   *c.* used up   *d.* filled up

2 The number of wild animals in this forest didn't <u>increase</u>.

    a. grow   *b.* match   *c.* return   *d.* change

C Choose the best word to complete each sentence.

1 There's only one _____ of pie left. Let's cut it in half.

    a. chip   *b.* piece   *c.* result   *d.* pair

2 David's parents _____ him to become a successful writer.

    a. try   *b.* worry   *c.* expect   *d.* appear

3 A huge hole has been _____ in the ozone layer.

    a. created   *b.* raised   *c.* arrived   *d.* broken

4 I didn't _____ who the boy was until he came up close to me.

    a. call   *b.* inform   *c.* ignore   *d.* realize

Unit ★ 09

ECONOMY

A Connect each word to its correct definition.

1 appealing or pleasing • • *a.* curious

2 wanting to know more about something • • *b.* promote

3 to make something more popular by advertising • • *c.* attention

4 the interest someone shows towards something • • *d.* attractive

B Write the word that has the opposite meaning of each word.

cheap	messy	success	weakness

1 clean : _____ *2* failure : _____

3 strength : _____ *4* expensive : _____

★ *The Hans Brinker Hotel*

Many companies want to look attractive to customers. So they try to show only the advantages of their products. However, one hotel in the Netherlands is different. It gets people's attention by _____(A)_____.

5　　The Hans Brinker Hotel is a cheap and well-located hotel for travelers. It just provides a room with a bed — nothing special. But the hotel managers don't promote it by saying that it's cheap or it's in a good location. Instead, they focus on all its bad points. They proudly advertise the hotel's poor facilities and service. In the ads, <u>broken chairs, chipped forks, and messy beds</u> are shown. And they also say, "It can't get any worse, but we'll do our

10　best." What's the result? Many young travelers become curious about the hotel and want to stay there. Now, it is one of the most popular hotels in the Netherlands!

　　So, do you want to catch people's attention and become successful? Then think differently from others and try something new. <u>This can be a key</u>

15　<u>to success.</u>

1 What is the best title for the passage?

　a. The Power of Advertisements
　b. Visit the World's Worst Hotel!
　c. A Unique and Successful Hotel Ad
　d. Some Ways to Choose the Best Hotel

2 What is the best choice for blank (A)?

    a. using famous people

    b. advertising its good points

    c. honestly showing its weaknesses

    d. providing people with good service

3 Why does the hotel show <u>broken chairs, chipped forks, and messy beds</u> in its ads?

    a. to create a clean image

    b. to describe its popularity

    c. to show how bad it really is

    d. to introduce its long history

4 How do the hotel's ads affect many young travelers?

_____

5 What does the underlined sentence mean?

    a. Many people are afraid to try new things.

    b. Advertising is the only way to be successful.

    c. Doing what others don't do can lead to success.

    d. Being unique can't draw people's attention anymore.

STRATEGIC SUMMARY

Fill in the blanks with the correct words.

Ads for the Hans Brinker Hotel are different from most hotel ads. They don't focus on the _____ parts of the hotel. Rather, they honestly show all the _____ that the hotel has. It might seem strange, but these ads make people _____ about it. As a result, it has become one of the most _____ hotels in the Netherlands.

> nice   negative   well-known   curious   problems

VOCABULARY REVIEW

A Write the correct word next to its definition.

focus	result	facility	traveler	broken

1 a person who is traveling: _____

2 to pay close attention to something: _____

3 something that happens due to previous events: _____

4 something like a room or equipment given to people to use: _____

B Find the word that has a similar meaning to the underlined word.

1 The witness <u>honestly</u> told the police what he saw.

   a. badly   *b.* quietly   *c.* frankly   *d.* proudly

2 One <u>advantage</u> of this computer is that it's very easy to use.

   a. benefit   *b.* increase   *c.* influence   *d.* weakness

C Choose the best word to complete each sentence.

1 We need to _____ our products in the paper to increase sales.

   a. create   *b.* protect   *c.* produce   *d.* advertise

2 The school will _____ free supplies for its students in need.

   a. ban   *b.* sell   *c.* trade   *d.* provide

3 My apartment is in a good _____. It's close to a subway station.

   a. city   *b.* field   *c.* location   *d.* condition

4 Everyone in this restaurant is very kind, so it is famous for its _____.

   a. food   *b.* service   *c.* prices   *d.* specialty

Unit ★ 10

JOBS

A Connect each word to its correct definition.

1 to hit something hard with your fist • • *a.* match

2 a device that makes your voice louder • • *b.* punch

3 a person who guides the making of a film or play • • *c.* director

4 to cause something to fit well with something else • • *d.* microphone

B Write the word that has the opposite meaning of each word.

complete create add real

1 fake : _____

2 start : _____

3 destroy : _____

4 take away : _____

★ *An Interview with a Foley Artist*

It's not just actors and directors who play a part in making films. There are people with other jobs behind the scenes, including Foley artists. Amy Parker, a Hollywood Foley artist, is here with us.

Q: What do Foley artists do?

5   **A:** Our job is to create sound effects for movies. (①) We create sounds that we often miss in our daily lives, like the sound of footsteps or an opening door. (②) For instance, we create the laser sword sound in science fiction movies like *Star Wars*. (③) These sound effects make movies seem more real. (④)

10   **Q:** I see. But for the actual sounds, don't directors just record them while making a film?

A: Not really. Because the microphones are usually set up to record the actors' words, they can't pick up other sounds well. So they need us to add those sounds after they complete filming.

15   **Q:** _____(A)_____

A: We work in a studio with a big screen. While a film plays on the screen, we add sound effects, matching the timing of the action. We create the sounds by using interesting objects. Can you guess how we make a punching sound? We hit a

20   watermelon!

READING COMPREHENSION

1   What is the interview mainly about?

    a.   Hollywood voice actors

    b.   The history of Foley arts

    c.   Professional sound artists

    d.   Technologies in filmmaking

2 Where would the following sentence best fit?

> We even make sounds that don't exist in this world.

a. ①   b. ②   c. ③   d. ④

3 Which of the following is NOT a sound that Foley artists would make?

a. The sound of a tornado
b. The sound of a car crashing
c. The sound of an actor singing
d. The sound of an actor running

4 Why can't the microphones pick up every sound while filming?

Because _____ .

5 What is the best choice for blank (A)?

a. What tools do you use?
b. How do you do your job?
c. Why did you decide to be a Foley artist?
d. What were some of your favorite scenes?

STRATEGIC SUMMARY

Fill in the blanks with the correct words.

Foley artists make the _____ for movies. They make sounds that we often miss in our daily lives as well as _____ ones. Sound effects are needed because the _____ are usually focused on the actors' voices. Foley artists add the sounds while watching the movie in a studio. They _____ the sounds perfectly with the action. They sometimes use fun things to make these sounds.

> objects   match   microphones   sound effects   non-existing

VOCABULARY REVIEW

A Complete the sentences with the words in the box. (Change the form if needed.)

studio	sword	timing	actual	film

1 The director planned to _____ a documentary.

2 This is a(n) _____ where music recordings are made.

3 He looks very young, but nobody knows his _____ age.

4 It's bad _____ to go talk to Mom. She is very angry now.

B Find the word that has a similar meaning to the underlined word.

1 The couple <u>set up</u> a new stereo in the living room.

    a. cleaned   *b.* moved   *c.* installed   *d.* broke down

2 Ashley doesn't talk much; she <u>seems</u> like a serious person.

    a. thinks   *b.* looks   *c.* works   *d.* talks

C Choose the best word to complete each sentence.

1 Henry _____ me in the face, so I got a bloody nose.

    a. looked   *b.* hit   *c.* took   *d.* stamped

2 Many people want to know whether life _____ on Mars.

    a. exists   *b.* stands   *c.* watches   *d.* counts

3 The children walked slowly to hear their _____ in the snow.

    a. knocks   *b.* thunder   *c.* footsteps   *d.* raindrops

4 I always _____ my professor's lectures so that I don't miss anything.

    a. skip   *b.* accept   *c.* trust   *d.* record

Unit ★ 11

FESTIVALS

A Connect each word to its correct definition.

1 to show respect to someone • • *a.* bull

2 an adult male member of the cattle family • • *b.* route

3 a way or road to go from one place to another • • *c.* honor

4 a device that explodes into colorful lights in the sky • • *d.* firework

B Write the word that has the opposite meaning of each word.

thrilling throw explosive behind

1 quiet : _____   *2* boring : _____

3 catch : _____   *4* ahead of : _____

★ *The Festival of San Fermin*

Have you heard of the festival of San Fermin? It's held in Pamplona, Spain from the 6th to the 14th of July every year. <u>The festival was started to honor the first Bishop of Pamplona, Saint Fermin.</u> I took

5　part in the festival last July. Let me tell you about my fascinating experience there!

　　The festival began at noon with the firing of a rocket. At the sound of loud, explosive "bang," participants started to throw wine at each other. Of course,

10　I was all wet, but I had lots of fun.

　　During the festival, I watched parades, concerts, flamenco dancing, and fireworks. But the most exciting part was the running of the bulls. Six bulls are made to run an 825-meter route to the *bullring. Hundreds of people run with them. Because the run only takes three minutes, I thought it would be a

15　piece of cake. However, I got scared when I saw a large bull right behind me. So I ran as fast as I could. This was the most thrilling experience of my life!

*bullring: a place to watch bullfighting

READING COMPREHENSION

1　What is the passage mainly about?

   a.　The world's largest bull market

   b.　Interesting races at Spanish festivals

   c.　The history of the festival of San Fermin

   d.　A happy memory at a festival in Pamplona

2 What can be inferred from the underlined sentence?

    a. Saint Fermin died in July.

    b. A bishop started the festival.

    c. The festival was named after a bishop.

    d. Saint Fermin was the first Spanish bishop.

3 What is NOT mentioned about the festival of San Fermin?

    a. Where it is held

    b. How it became famous

    c. How long it lasts

    d. What events take place

4 Why did the writer think the running of the bulls would be easy?

Because _____ .

5 Who is NOT talking about his or her experience at the festival of San Fermin?

    a. Sam: I sprayed wine on people around me.

    b. Joan: Riding on big bulls was very exciting.

    c. Brian: I saw various parades and performances.

    d. David: It was great to watch the beautiful fireworks.

STRATEGIC SUMMARY

Fill in the blanks with the correct words.

The writer went to the festival of San Fermin in Spain last July. A _____ was shot into the air to start the festival. Then everyone _____ wine at each other. Parades, music, dancing, and fireworks were enjoyed at the festival. But the most exciting part was the running of the _____ . Even though it only took three minutes, the writer was _____ because a big bull was running behind him. However, he thought it was an amazing experience.

| bulls | scared | threw | rocket | fascinating |

VOCABULARY REVIEW

A Complete the sentences with the words in the box. (Change the form if needed.)

hold	take part in	rocket	participant	experience

1 The meeting will be _____ next week.

2 He is the oldest _____ in this marathon.

3 She _____ the talent show and won first prize.

4 Failing the exam was a very painful _____ for me.

B Find the word that has a similar meaning to the underlined word.

1 Solving such puzzles is a <u>piece of cake</u> for him.

   a. problem   *b.* easy task   *c.* special treat   *d.* cheap dessert

2 She was so <u>scared</u> that she couldn't ride the horse.

   a. sick   *b.* tired   *c.* young   *d.* afraid

C Choose the best word to complete each sentence.

1 The movie was _____. I wanted to see it again.

   a. uninteresting   *b.* boring   *c.* terrible   *d.* fascinating

2 A big _____ was held to welcome the national soccer team.

   a. parade   *b.* statue   *c.* uniform   *d.* public

3 By car, it _____ two hours to go from here to my hometown.

   a. pays   *b.* sends   *c.* takes   *d.* spends

4 The bookstore's actually _____ next to my office.

   a. under   *b.* before   *c.* left   *d.* right

Unit ★ 12

SOCIETY

A Connect each word to its correct definition.

1 having no place to live • • *a.* issue

2 the outside part of a book • • *b.* cover

3 a thin book with many articles and pictures • • *c.* homeless

4 an important topic which people talk about • • *d.* magazine

B Write the word that has a similar meaning to each word.

impact donate common talent

1 gift : _____ *2* give : _____

3 effect : _____ *4* ordinary : _____

★ *The Big Issue*

Have you ever read *The Big Issue*? It's a common street magazine, except that it's sold by homeless people.

The Big Issue was founded by two English businessmen in 1991. They wanted to help poor people who were living on the streets of London. But

5 they didn't just give them money. Instead, they offered them chances to

_____(A)_____. As magazine vendors, they get the magazines for £1.25 each and sell them for £2.50.

So, what does *The Big Issue* deal with? Like other magazines, its articles include interviews with stars, movie reviews, and global issues. What makes

10 it special is that people donate their talents for the magazine. The writers and designers don't get paid for their work. And celebrities like David Beckham work as cover models for free.

As its title indicates, the magazine addresses a "big issue," and it has had a great social impact. It has made people think about the issue of homelessness. It is now sold in ten countries, and people help the homeless by buying it.

READING COMPREHENSION

1 What is the best title for the passage?

   a. Build a Place for Homeless People

   b. Get a Special Street Magazine for Free

   c. *The Big Issue*: Real Help for Homeless People

   d. *The Big Issue*: A Perfect Magazine for Businessmen

2 What is the best choice for blank (A)?

    a. think about social issues

    b. make money by working

    c. donate money for the homeless

    d. write their stories in the magazine

3 What can be inferred from the 3rd paragraph?

    a. Many people want to work for *The Big Issue*.

    b. People like *The Big Issue* because of its articles.

    c. People who make *The Big Issue* don't work for money.

    d. People who donate money can get *The Big Issue* for free.

4 How has *The Big Issue* affected society?

_____

5 What is NOT true about *The Big Issue*?

    a. Homeless people sell it on the street.

    b. The English government first started it in 1991.

    c. Vendors can make £1.25 by selling one magazine.

    d. Its articles are similar to those of other magazines.

STRATEGIC ORGANIZER

Fill in the blanks with the correct words.

The Big Issue

The start
- It was started to help the _____.
- The vendors sell the _____ and make money.

Why it is special
- Many people _____ their talents to make the magazine.

Its social impact
- People have become interested in the _____ of homelessness.

> free   issue   donate   homeless   magazine

★ ★ ★
VOCABULARY REVIEW

A Write the correct word next to its definition.

| found | special | article | vendor | celebrity |

1 a famous person: _____

2 to start an organization, company, etc.: _____

3 a piece of writing in a newspaper or magazine: _____

4 someone who sells things, usually on the street: _____

B Find the word that has a similar meaning to the underlined word.

1 The global economy has been gradually improving.

   a. local   b. social   c. national   d. international

2 We will do our best to offer great service.

   a. charge   b. provide   c. spend   d. produce

C Choose the best word to complete each sentence.

1 This is your last _____ to get a discount. Don't miss it.

   a. goal   b. chance   c. speech   d. business

2 The ingredients for this bread _____ flour, eggs, and butter.

   a. give   b. make   c. include   d. address

3 She is a part-timer, and she gets _____ about 5 dollars an hour.

   a. paid   b. sent   c. helped   d. donated

4 Before I choose a movie to watch, I usually read _____ of it.

   a. books   b. reviews   c. directors   d. interviews

HUMAN BODY

★ ──── VOCABULARY PREVIEW ──── ★

A Connect each word to its correct definition.

1 usual or ordinary • • *a.* stretch

2 to become bigger or longer • • *b.* normal

3 to eat more food than your body needs • • *c.* stomach

4 the organ where digestion mostly takes place • • *d.* overeat

B Write the word that has the opposite meaning of each word.

remember   keep   fill   finish

1 stop : _____

2 begin : _____

3 empty : _____

4 forget : _____

★ The Human Stomach

Imagine you have just eaten a large meal at a restaurant. You feel very full, but the waiter brings you some cheesecake for free. A moment ago, you felt like you couldn't eat anymore. But you eat the cheesecake anyway!

How are you able to eat more when your stomach already feels full?

5 You can do this because the human stomach _____(A)_____.
It grows larger or smaller, depending on how much you eat. Usually, the human stomach is about 12 inches long, 6 inches wide, and can hold a liter of food. But when you eat a lot, it can stretch like a balloon to hold two liters or more! Then, after you finish eating, it slowly gets smaller and returns to its
10 normal size again.

However, if you overeat all the time, your stomach will keep growing. Then, you have to eat more food to fill it. This can make you overweight. So remember to treat your stomach well. The fact that you can eat more doesn't mean that you should.

READING COMPREHENSION

1 What is the passage mainly about?

  a. Why we eat three meals a day
  b. Benefits of having smaller meals
  c. Ways to keep your stomach small
  d. How big the human stomach can be

2 How does the writer introduce the topic?

    a. by making a funny joke

    b. by giving background information

    c. by giving an example of a situation

    d. by talking about his or her own experience

3 What is the best choice for blank (A)?

    a. works slowly

    b. changes in size

    c. is hard and strong

    d. has good bacteria in it

4 Why can we get overweight if our stomach keeps growing?

Because _____.

5 What is NOT true about the human stomach?

    a. It's about 12 inches long.

    b. It can usually hold about a liter of food.

    c. Once it stretches, it never becomes smaller again.

    d. It's not good for your health to let your stomach grow too much.

STRATEGIC SUMMARY

Fill in the blanks with the correct words.

Even when you feel _____, you can usually keep eating. This is because the human stomach can get bigger when necessary. Normally, it can hold about one liter of food. But when you eat more, it can _____ to hold more than two liters. Later, it _____ to its original size. But if you keep overeating, your stomach won't have a chance to get smaller. This can cause you to become _____.

| finish | full | stretch | overweight | returns |

VOCABULARY REVIEW

★ ★ ★

A Complete the sentences with the words in the box. (Change the form if needed.)

| depend | treat | for free | mean | overweight |

1 She is _____, so she should exercise more.

2 Can you explain what you _____ by "last chance"?

3 I don't like the way he _____ me. He acts like I'm a baby.

4 Download the software _____ today. Starting tomorrow, you have to pay.

B Find the word that has a similar meaning to the underlined word.

1 It would be safer to go home now. It's <u>growing</u> dark.

　　a. becoming 　　 *b.* aging 　　　 *c.* losing 　　　 *d.* improving

2 How much water can this bottle <u>hold</u>?

　　a. spend 　　　 *b.* pour 　　　 *c.* make 　　　 *d.* contain

C Choose the best word to complete each sentence.

1 Take this medicine three times a day, 30 minutes after _____.

　　a. cooks 　　　 *b.* meats 　　　 *c.* meals 　　　 *d.* deals

2 Would you wait for a _____? I'll come back in five minutes.

　　a. lifetime 　　 *b.* moment 　　 *c.* movement 　　 *d.* stop

3 After the party is over, their lives _____ to normal.

　　a. expect 　　　 *b.* memorize 　　 *c.* return 　　　 *d.* agree

4 Newspapers have a duty to provide their readers with the _____.

　　a. facts .　 *b.* profits 　　　 *c.* fiction 　　　 *d.* rumors

NATURE

★ ── VOCABULARY PREVIEW ── ★

A Connect each word to its correct definition.

1 to grow bigger or stronger ·   · **a.** chase

2 to follow someone or something quickly ·   · **b.** vehicle

3 a machine for transporting people or goods ·   · **c.** storm

4 a weather event marked by strong winds and heavy rain · · **d.** develop

B Write the word that has the opposite meaning of each word.

violent   risky   professional   rare

1 safe : _____   *2* calm : _____

3 common : _____   *4* amateur : _____

★ Storm Chasing

Storms can be very dangerous, so it's best to stay away from them. But some people, called storm chasers, look for storms. Tom Hale, a professional storm chaser, is here to tell us about storm chasing.

Q: What do storm chasers do?

5 **A:** Basically, we follow storms. (①) And then we watch, record, and take pictures of them. (②) Why do we do this? (③) Many others, like me, do it to study and provide information about storms, such as when and how they form. (④)

Q: Can you explain how storms form?

10 **A:** When warm, wet air meets cold air, these two different air masses push against each other. This creates a violent movement of air with heavy rain, lightning, and thunder. This is how storms happen.

Q: What kind of equipment do storm chasers use?

A: We use high-tech equipment _____(A)_____. For example,
15 satellite maps show us where a storm is developing, and GPS systems help us follow the storm. When we are close to the storm, a specially designed vehicle protects us from any dangers outside.

Q: _____(B)_____

A: Storm chasing may sound risky. But moments of capturing nature's rare
20 beauty are unforgettable. If you happen to see these wonderful sights, you might want to chase storms, too!

READING COMPREHENSION

1 What is the interview mainly about?

a. doing an unusual job
b. predicting the weather
c. preparing for dangerous storms
d. developing a technology for storm chasing

2 Where would the following sentence best fit?

> Some chase storms simply out of interest.

a. ①   *b.* ②   *c.* ③   *d.* ④

3 What happens when warm, wet air and cold air meet?

_____

4 What is the best choice for blank (A)?

a. to move fast
b. to form storms
c. to find where a storm is
d. to stay safe from extreme weather

5 What is the best choice for blank (B)?

a. What makes storm chasing risky?
b. What attracts you to storm chasing?
c. When did you first start storm chasing?
d. What was your best moment as a storm chaser?

STRATEGIC SUMMARY

Fill in the blanks with the correct words.

Storm chasers _____ storms to watch and record them. Storms happen when two different air masses meet. Storm chasers use different kinds of _____ to chase storms, such as satellite maps and GPS systems. And to _____ themselves from outside dangers, they use a specially designed vehicle. Although storm chasing can be risky, storm chasers keep chasing storms to _____ the beautiful moments of nature.

> capture   equipment   follow   protect   lightning

★ ★ ★
VOCABULARY REVIEW

A Complete the sentences with the words in the box. (Change the form if needed.)

| mass | capture | satellite | equipment | danger |

1 Do you know how many _____ are circling the earth?

2 Global warming is a serious _____ to our environment.

3 The incident was _____ by CCTV cameras inside the building.

4 When you ride a bicycle, you should wear safety _____, like a helmet.

B Find the word that has a similar meaning to the underlined word.

1 I witnessed an amazing <u>sight</u> as soon as I entered the room.

    a. scene   *b.* place   *c.* sign   *d.* feeling

2 Our trip to Australia was an <u>unforgettable</u> and enjoyable experience.

    a. familiar   *b.* typical   *c.* important   *d.* memorable

C Choose the best word to complete each sentence.

1 I'll show you the way. Please _____ me.

    a. fold   *b.* close   *c.* follow   *d.* leave

2 These trees help to _____ my house from the wind.

    a. protect   *b.* push   *c.* stay   *d.* lift

3 We need a really exciting idea to _____ people's attention.

    a. sell   *b.* attract   *c.* count   *d.* pick

4 Where is Henry? We have been _____ him for hours.

    a. talking with   *b.* caring for   *c.* meeting with   *d.* looking for

Unit ★ 15

WORLD

A Connect each word to its correct definition.

1 to try to win a game, contest, etc. •   • *a.* tribe

2 to put something on or over something else •   • *b.* cover

3 a person who decides who wins in a contest •   • *c.* judge

4 a group of people who live in an area and share •   • *d.* compete
the same customs

B Write the word that has the opposite meaning of each word.

single	strength	winner	thin

1 thick : _____)

2 loser : _____

3 married : _____

4 weakness : _____

★ *The Wodaabe Tribe*

10

Which is more important for men, beauty or strength? For the men of the Wodaabe tribe of western and central Africa, beauty is! That's because beautiful men are more successful at getting girlfriends or wives. Once a year, they even compete in a festival called Gerewol to see who is the most beautiful.

So what features do the Wodaabe consider to be beautiful? Lighter skin color, a thin nose, a tall and slim body, and white teeth are all essential. At the ceremony, the men cover their face with yellow and red powder, and they draw a white line on their nose. They also dance and open their mouths
15 wide to show their teeth.

At the end of the event, judges decide who wins. ① These judges are single Wodaabe women who are chosen for their beauty. ② People shouldn't be judged by their looks. ③ The lucky winner is admired for years in the tribe. ④ But that's not all. The winner also has a chance to marry the most
20 beautiful woman in the tribe!

READING COMPREHENSION

1 What is the passage mainly about?

   a. A beauty contest for men

   b. Various standards of beauty

   c. How Africans decorate themselves

   d. A wedding ceremony of the Wodaabe tribe

2 Why is beauty important for the men of the Wodaabe tribe?

Because _____ .

3 What can be inferred about the men from the underlined part?

    a. They are not happy with their looks.

    b. They try to show their best features.

    c. They are not beautiful without make-up.

    d. They have to spend a lot of money for the event.

4 Which sentence is NOT needed in the passage?

    a. ①   *b.* ②   *c.* ③   *d.* ④

5 What is NOT mentioned about the beauty contest in the Gerewol festival?

    a. How often it is held

    b. What the beauty standards are

    c. How old contestants should be

    d. Who decides the winner

STRATEGIC ORGANIZER

Fill in the blanks with the correct words.

The beauty contest of the Wodaabe tribe
- Once a year, the Wodaabe men _____ to be the most beautiful.

The beauty _____
- They think light skin, a thin nose, a slender body, and white teeth are important.

The _____ for the winner
- Single women chosen for their beauty pick the winner.
- The winner is admired for years.
- He has a chance to _____ the most beautiful tribe woman.

| marry | standards | compete | prize | ceremony |

VOCABULARY REVIEW

★ ★ ★

A Write the correct word next to its definition.

skin	consider	draw	light	powder

1 pale in color, not dark: _____

2 the outer layer of a person's body: _____

3 to think of something in a particular way: _____

4 a fine, dry substance that looks like dust or sand: _____

B Find the word that has a similar meaning to the underlined word.

1 Teaching experience is <u>essential</u> for this job.

   a. new   *b.* better   *c.* helpful   *d.* necessary

2 Tina's mother is very beautiful. Tina has her mother's good <u>looks</u>.

   a. eyes   *b.* appearance   *c.* character   *d.* health

C Choose the best word to complete each sentence.

1 Julie is _____ by her classmates for her friendly and polite attitude.

   a. taught   *b.* brought   *c.* shown   *d.* admired

2 Exercising regularly helps him to keep _____.

   a. slim   *b.* lazy   *c.* busy   *d.* weak

3 You can _____ between these two topics.

   a. cause   *b.* divide   *c.* refuse   *d.* choose

4 He finally left because I was not _____ in changing his mind.

   a. proud   *b.* friendly   *c.* successful   *d.* common

Unit ★ 16
TRAVEL

★ ——— VOCABULARY PREVIEW ——— ★

A Connect each word to its correct definition.

1 to harm or break something •   • *a.* exotic

2 animals living in natural conditions •   • *b.* wildlife

3 influenced by special magic powers •   • *c.* damage

4 unusual because it comes from far away •   • *d.* enchanted

B Write the word that has the opposite meaning of each word.

protect   foreign   fearless   imaginary

1 real : _____   *2* native : _____

3 destroy : _____   *4* cowardly : _____

★ The Galapagos Islands

Have you heard about the Enchanted Islands? They are not an imaginary place in a fairy tale. They are the Galapagos Islands in the Pacific Ocean.

As the islands are 1,000 km away from South America, they
5 have barely been touched by humans. Because of this, they are home to some unique wildlife. Once you step on the islands, their exotic animals will welcome you. (①) You will come face to face with dancing blue-footed boobies and small Galapagos penguins. (②) Even shy animals like lava lizards won't run away from you. (③) So you
10 can see them up close. (④) You can even swim just inches away from a cute baby sea lion.

However, to protect this beautiful place, there are some rules tourists should follow. Don't disturb the wildlife. Basically, you can't touch or feed the animals. Also, you must not bring along foreign animals. They can damage
15 the *ecosystem of the islands.

Now, are you ready to take a special vacation in the Galapagos Islands? It will be a once-in-a-lifetime experience!

*ecosystem: all the plants and animals that live together in a certain area

1 What is the best title for the passage?

    a. The Best Plan for Your Summer Vacation

    b. The Deadly Animals of the Galapagos Islands

    c. A Place of Natural Beauty: The Galapagos Islands

    d. The Galapagos Islands: Its Discovery and Development

READING COMPREHENSION

2 Why does this place have such unique wildlife?

Because it is far away, _____.

3 Where would the following sentence best fit?

> What's more, the animals on these islands are famous for being fearless toward humans.

a. ① *b.* ② *c.* ③ *d.* ④

4 Who broke the rules of the Galapagos Islands?

a. Claire: I swam with a giant turtle at the beach.
b. Peter: I didn't bring my puppy to the islands even though I wanted to.
c. Jenny: I gave some cookies to the penguins because they looked hungry.
d. Jason: When the lizards came towards me, I just stood there without touching them.

5 What does the underlined sentence mean?

a. There is little time left to travel to the islands.
b. Everyone must visit the Galapagos Islands at least once.
c. Visiting the Galapagos Islands will be an amazing experience.
d. You wouldn't want to go to the Galapagos Islands more than once.

STRATEGIC SUMMARY

Fill in the blanks with the correct words.

The Galapagos Islands are known for their _____ beauty. They are far away from the nearest land, so humans have barely touched them. Because of this, the animals on the Galapagos Islands are very special. They aren't _____ of humans, so they won't run away from you. But visitors must obey some _____. You must not touch or feed the animals. And in order to protect their ecosystem, you can't _____ other animals to the Galapagos Islands.

> afraid   natural   bring   rules   vacation

VOCABULARY REVIEW

A Complete the sentences with the words in the box. (Change the form if needed.)

rule	disturb	shy	feed	barely

1 Jamie and I are not close friends. I _____ know him.

2 Don't _____ the people sleeping by turning on the light.

3 You must not _____ the animals in the zoo. The food can make them sick.

4 My cat is so _____ that he hides under a blanket when someone comes to visit.

B Find the word that has a similar meaning to the underlined word.

1 Noah has a <u>unique</u> ability to communicate with animals.

    a. real   *b.* special   *c.* common   *d.* familiar

2 Good sportsmanship is about <u>following</u> the rules of the game.

    a. breaking   *b.* carrying   *c.* keeping   *d.* celebrating

C Choose the best word to complete each sentence.

1 Let's meet _____. I'm tired of talking on the phone.

    a. hand in hand   *b.* face to face   *c.* step by step   *d.* shoulder to shoulder

2 If you come across a fierce dog, stay still and never _____.

    a. run away   *b.* look out   *c.* work out   *d.* get over

3 Hawaii is a group of _____ located in the central Pacific Ocean.

    a. rivers   *b.* islands   *c.* beaches   *d.* mountains

4 I was upset because he didn't apologize to me for _____ on my foot.

    a. helping   *b.* looking   *c.* lifting   *d.* stepping

Unit ★ 17
TEENS

A Connect each word to its correct definition.

1 to keep something secret   •   • *a.* hurt

2 to have an effect on something   •   • *b.* hide

3 to have or use something with others   •   • *c.* share

4 to cause damage to something or someone   •   • *d.* affect

B Write the word that has a similar meaning to each word.

moreover	trust	private	upset

1 belief : _____

2 angry : _____

3 personal : _____

4 furthermore : _____

★ Brian's Problem

Before Reading
Do you think sharing everything is good for a relationship?

Dear Dr. Phil,

My girlfriend wants to know the passwords for my email and cellphone. But I don't want to tell her because they are private. What should I do?

5

Brian

Dear Brian,

Your girlfriend may think that a couple should share everything. You don't have to tell her your passwords if you don't want to. But you should give

10 her your reasons for wanting privacy. Otherwise, she may think you're hiding something from her.

Trust is very important in a relationship. However, reading private messages can often cause misunderstandings. And this can make you lose trust towards each other. Moreover, it doesn't affect just the two of you.

15 _____(A)_____, too. For example, your friends may be upset to know that your girlfriend reads their messages to you.

If you give her your passwords, she will be happy for a while. But later, it can hurt your relationship with her and your friends. So, you need to explain your reasons, and then she will understand. Remember, honesty is the best policy.

Dr. Phil

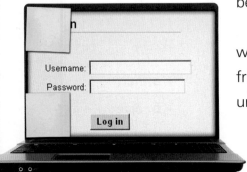

READING COMPREHENSION

1 What is Brian's problem in the passage?

a. Someone stole his passwords.

b. He wants to hide his weak points from his girlfriend.

c. His girlfriend often reads private messages on his phone.

d. He doesn't want to share his passwords with his girlfriend.

74

2 Why should Brian tell his girlfriend his reasons for wanting privacy?

If he doesn't give reasons, _____ .

3 What is the best choice for blank (A)?

a. It will hurt your girlfriend's feelings

b. You can learn more about each other's lives

c. You might invade the privacy of other people

d. It can affect the trust between you and your girlfriend

4 What does the underlined part mean?

a. It is always best to say how you really feel.

b. Telling a lie sometimes makes things better.

c. You can't always be honest with other people.

d. It is easy for couples to be honest with each other.

5 What is Brian NOT likely to tell his girlfriend?

a. We need to trust each other as a couple.

b. I think misunderstandings can hurt our relationship.

c. We can have a better relationship by sharing everything.

d. My friends will be angry if you read the emails they send to me.

STRATEGIC SUMMARY

Fill in the blanks with the correct words.

Brian wrote a letter to Dr. Phil, asking for advice. Brian's girlfriend wants to know his _____ . Brian is uncomfortable with this, so he's not sure what to do. Dr. Phil tells Brian that he should explain why he doesn't want to _____ his passwords. He says _____ is important in a relationship, and sharing private information might hurt it. Furthermore, sharing passwords can _____ other people's privacy, too.

trust	share	affect	explain	passwords

VOCABULARY REVIEW

★ ★ ★

A Write the correct word next to its definition.

password	misunderstanding	explain	policy	cause

1 to make something happen: _____

2 a situation in which something isn't understood correctly: _____

3 to tell someone about something to help them understand: _____

4 a private code you need in order to use a computer system: _____

B Find the word that has the opposite meaning of the underlined word.

1 May I use your computer <u>for a while</u>?

    a. in short   *b.* in brief   *c.* for a moment   *d.* for a long time

2 Jessica tried not to <u>lose</u> confidence at the speaking contest.

    a. find   *b.* make   *c.* fail   *d.* affect

C Choose the best word to complete each sentence.

1 The _____ was married and went on their honeymoon.

    a. twin   *b.* couple   *c.* family   *d.* crowd

2 You should leave now. _____, you'll be late for school.

    a. So   *b.* Therefore   *c.* Thus   *d.* Otherwise

3 You shouldn't lie to John. He thinks _____ is very important.

    a. policy   *b.* reason   *c.* honesty   *d.* friendship

4 He wanted some _____, so he closed the door.

    a. trust   *b.* privacy   *c.* messages   *d.* relationship

HISTORY

A Connect each word to its correct definition.

1 to arrive at a place · · *a.* reach

2 a person who uses a ship to explore · · *b.* discover

3 any of the earth's main areas of land · · *c.* navigator

4 to be the first person to know about something · · *d.* continent

B Write the word that has a similar meaning to each word.

nearly   evidence   realize   name

1 call : _____

2 proof : _____

3 almost : _____

4 notice : _____

★ *Who Discovered America?*

"Christopher Columbus discovered America in 1492." Many people think this is a fact. But did he

5 really? Some people don't agree with this idea. Here are their reasons.

First, there were people who

10 _____(A)_____.

Think about the Native Americans. They had already been living there since their ancestors moved across from Asia around 12,000 years ago. Second, Columbus was not even the first European to reach America. Scientists found evidence that the Vikings had been in the northern part of America. They

15 guess these Northern Europeans came to America nearly 500 years before Columbus. _____(B)_____, when Columbus arrived in America, he didn't even know where he was. He thought he was in eastern India. For that reason, Native Americans were called "Indians."

In fact, it was another navigator, Amerigo Vespucci, who realized that

20 this was a "New World." That's why the American continents are named after him. However, Columbus was the person who brought Europeans' attention to America. Maybe that's why many people believe that he discovered America.

READING COMPREHENSION

1 What is the passage mainly about?

 a. America and other new worlds

 b. Great European explorers in history

 c. How Christopher Columbus discovered America

 d. Some unfamiliar facts about the discovery of America

2 What is the best choice for blank (A)?

a. proved that Columbus didn't exist

b. lied about Columbus' achievement

c. helped Columbus discover America

d. found America earlier than Columbus

3 What is the best choice for blank (B)?

a. Yet

b. However

c. Moreover

d. Therefore

4 Why did Columbus call Native Americans "Indians"?

Because _____.

5 What is NOT true according to the passage?

a. The first Americans moved from Asia to America.

b. Columbus was the first European to find America.

c. America was named after Amerigo Vespucci.

d. Europeans became interested in America because of Columbus.

STRATEGIC SUMMARY

Fill in the blanks with the correct words.

Many people believe that Christopher Columbus _____ America in 1492. But in fact, Native Americans had already been living there when he arrived. And Columbus wasn't even the first _____ to visit America. Vikings were there hundreds of years before him. What's more, Columbus thought he was in _____, which is why he called the native people "Indians." A man named Amerigo Vespucci realized Columbus was _____. That's why the New World was named after him.

| European | wrong | India | discovered | navigator |

★ ★ ★
VOCABULARY REVIEW

A Write the correct word next to its definition.

| ancestor | scientist | eastern | believe | agree |

1 to think that something is true: _____

2 someone who does scientific research: _____

3 a person from whom you are descended: _____

4 to have the same opinion as someone else: _____

B Find the word that has the opposite meaning of the underlined word.

1 Call me when you arrive at the station. I'll pick you up.

　　 a. visit 　　　　 *b.* come 　　　　 *c.* leave 　　　　 *d.* close

2 A reporter should write articles using only facts.

　　 a. truth 　　　　 *b.* events 　　　　 *c.* actions 　　　　 *d.* fiction

C Choose the best word to complete each sentence.

1 I tried to reserve a ticket for the concert, but they were _____ sold out.

　　 a. exactly 　　　 *b.* enough 　　　 *c.* already 　　　 *d.* carefully

2 My family will _____ to Seoul from Busan next week.

　　 a. stay 　　　 *b.* move 　　　 *c.* stop 　　　 *d.* bring

3 James knocked on the table to get her _____.

　　 a. attitude 　　　 *b.* condition 　　　 *c.* attention 　　　 *d.* presentation

4 Tina looked very young, so I _____ her age was 14 or 15.

　　 a. knew 　　　 *b.* guessed 　　　 *c.* dreamed 　　　 *d.* chose

Unit ★ 19

ENVIRONMENT

★ *Urban Mining*

Each year, thousands of tons of electronic waste, including old cellphones and computers, is thrown away. This not only wastes resources but also harms the environment. Fortunately, urban *mining can solve this problem.

Urban mining is a newly developed industry. It involves getting metals
5 like copper, silver, and even gold from old electronics. As its sources are materials in the city, it's called "urban" mining. How does it work? First, old electronics are collected and broken into small parts. And then they're processed in order to separate valuable metals. <u>Someday, these metals will be born again as brand-new products!</u>

10 Urban mining is becoming popular for two reasons. For one thing, it's more economical than real mining. In fact, there's 30 times more gold in a ton of cellphones than in a ton of rock. It also helps the environment. Through urban mining, we can recycle old electronic products and reuse precious natural resources. The more we develop urban mining, the healthier our environment will become!

*mining: the process of getting coal or metal from the earth

READING COMPREHENSION

1 **What is the best title for the passage?**

a. How to Make Electronic Products

b. The Benefits of Using Electronic Products

c. Environmental Problems of Electronic Waste

d. The New Way to Recycle Electronic Products

2 What are the problems of increasing electronic waste? (Choose two.)

    a. It is too old to reuse.

    b. There is no way to recycle it.

    c. Useful resources are just thrown away.

    d. It has bad effects on the environment.

3 Why does urban mining have "urban" in its name?

Because _____ .

4 What does the underlined sentence mean?

    a. All electronics are made with metals.

    b. New products easily replace old products.

    c. The metals are reused to make new products.

    d. More metals are needed to make more electronics.

5 What is the 3rd paragraph mainly about?

    a. How urban mining works

    b. Why recycling is important

    c. The benefits of urban mining

    d. How to become an urban miner

STRATEGIC ORGANIZER

Fill in the blanks with the correct words.

Urban Mining — An industry that involves getting metals from old _____ products

The process of urban mining
- Old electronics are _____ and broken into parts.
- After being processed, metals are separated from them.

Why urban mining is popular
- It's more _____ than real mining.
- It can make the environment _____ .

| healthier | products | gathered | electronic | economical |

★ ★ ★

VOCABULARY REVIEW

A Choose the correct word for each definition.

develop	valuable	resource	industry	recycle

1 very useful and important: _____

2 a particular type of economic activity: _____

3 something useful in nature, such as coal or oil: _____

4 to process used things in order to use them again: _____

B Find the word that has the opposite meaning of the underlined word.

1 His hobby is collecting precious paintings and jewels.

   a. safe   *b.* natural   *c.* worthless   *d.* expensive

2 If we waste water, we won't have clean water in the future.

   a. lose   *b.* save   *c.* spend   *d.* consume

C Choose the best word to complete each sentence.

1 Linda was tired of life in the _____, so she went to live in the country.

   a. job   *b.* city   *c.* park   *d.* backyard

2 Pollution of the sea can _____ marine life.

   a. harm   *b.* help   *c.* solve   *d.* become

3 You can _____ this glass bottle as a flower vase.

   a. reach   *b.* reuse   *c.* reduce   *d.* grow

4 This car runs for days with a small amount of gas, so it's very _____.

   a. diligent   *b.* ineffective   *c.* wasteful   *d.* economical

Unit ★ 20

CULTURE

A Connect each word to its correct definition.

1 twelve o'clock at night •

2 a particular type of food •

3 the feeling of being happy •

4 to try not to do something •

• *a.* dish

• *b.* avoid

• *c.* midnight

• *d.* happiness

B Write the word that has a similar meaning to each word.

welcome	prefer	beginning	rich

1 start : _____

2 greet : _____

3 wealthy : _____

4 like better : _____

★ *Foods for the New Year*

At the beginning of the year, people around the world welcome the New Year in different ways. One of them is to eat a special food that will _____(A)_____.

So, which foods do people eat? In Spain, people eat 12 grapes at midnight on New Year's Eve. People think eating 12 grapes will bring them happiness for 12 months. ① In Western Europe, people prefer green vegetables like cabbage. ② Green vegetables are good for your eyes. ③ These vegetables look like folded bills. ④ So people believe they can become rich by eating them. In some Asian countries, like China and Japan, people eat long noodles. They think that the long noodles symbolize long life.

However, there are also some foods people avoid around the New Year. For example, some people think their life might go in the wrong direction if they eat lobster. This is because lobsters move backward.

Whichever lucky dish you enjoy for the New Year, don't eat it too much. Otherwise, you'll have to start the New Year on a diet!

READING COMPREHENSION

1 What is the best title for the passage?

a. The Special Meaning of New Year's Eve

b. What Are Your New Year's Resolutions?

c. Celebrate the New Year with Lucky Foods!

d. New Year Food Festivals around the World

2 What is the best choice for blank (A)?

    a. keep you healthy

    b. make you feel pleased

    c. bring you good fortune

    d. help you forget the past

3 Which sentence is NOT needed in the passage?

    a. ①   *b.* ②   *c.* ③   *d.* ④

4 Why do some people avoid eating lobster?

Because _____ .

5 Which is NOT true according to the passage?

    a. In Spain, people believe eating 12 grapes will make them rich.

    b. In Western Europe, green vegetables stand for money.

    c. Some Asians believe they can live for a long time by eating noodles.

    d. Some people believe eating lobster brings bad luck.

STRATEGIC SUMMARY

Fill in the blanks with the correct words.

People from different cultures eat special foods to welcome the _____. They do this because they believe it will bring them good fortune. In Spain, people eat 12 grapes and hope to have 12 months of _____. In Western Europe, people eat green vegetables because they look like _____. They hope this will make them wealthy. Some Asians eat noodles because they represent long life. People also _____ some foods, like lobster, that they believe might bring bad luck.

> avoid   prefer   money   happiness   New Year

★ ★ ★
VOCABULARY REVIEW

A Choose the correct word for each definition.

fold	backward	eve	cabbage	direction

1 toward a position that is behind: _____

2 the night or day before an event: _____

3 to bend a piece of paper or cloth, etc.: _____

4 the course along which something moves: _____

B Find the word that has a similar meaning to the underlined word.

1 My father was driving on the <u>wrong</u> side of the road.

   a. different   *b.* incorrect   *c.* another   *d.* left

2 It was her good <u>fortune</u> to buy a computer at a cheap price.

   a. place   *b.* habit   *c.* chance   *d.* store

C Choose the best word to complete each sentence.

1 A four-leaf clover _____ good luck in almost every culture.

   a. feeds   *b.* realizes   *c.* bounces   *d.* symbolizes

2 Mike was _____ to win a million dollars in the lottery.

   a. lucky   *b.* tired   *c.* afraid   *d.* nervous

3 The _____ are so slippery that they're hard to eat with chopsticks.

   a. services   *b.* noodles   *c.* platters   *d.* bowls

4 He didn't have any _____ in his wallet, only a few coins.

   a. pens   *b.* bags   *c.* bills   *d.* brushes

Reading FORWARD

BASIC 1

★ Answer Key ★

Reading FORWARD

BASIC 1

★ Answer Key ★

VOCABULARY PREVIEW

A **1** a **2** d **3** b **4** c   B **1** giant **2** enter **3** amusing **4** reach

★ *The Corn Maze*

1 c **2** d **3** b **4** the corn was so tall that he couldn't see anything around him **5** b

---

나는 Andy이다. 오늘 나는 California의 Dixon에 있는 옥수수 미로에 갔다. 그것은 세계에서 가장 큰 옥수수 미로이다. 나는 미로의 크기에 매우 놀랐다. 그것은 200,000㎡가 넘는다! 그 미로는 가을 수확 철에 인기 있는 관광 명소이다. 많은 사람들이 들어가기 위해 줄을 서서 기다리고 있는 것을 보는 것은 즐거웠다.

바로 가까이서 보면, 미로는 그냥 키 큰 옥수수 식물의 밭처럼 보였다. 하지만 좀 더 높은 곳에서 나는 미로의 디자인을 볼 수 있었다. 올해 그것은 거대한 호박처럼 보이도록 설계되었다. 작년에는 자유의 여신상처럼 보였다고 들었다.

미로 안에서, 나는 지도를 가지고도 어디로 가야 할지 몰랐다. 옥수수는 너무 키가 커서 나는 주변의 어떤 것도 볼 수 없었다. 나는 거의 길을 잃었다! 두 시간 후에 나는 직원의 도움을 받아서 마침내 도착 지점에 도달했다.

미로를 탐험한 후에 나는 옥수수 목욕도 했는데, 그것은 옥수수 낟알로 가득 차 있었다. 이상한 느낌이었지만 좋았다! 나는 당신도 그 미로를 방문하기를 추천한다.

어휘   corn[kɔ:rn] 몡 옥수수   surprised[sərpráizd] 쥉 놀란   amusing[əmjú:ziŋ] 쥉 재미있는, 즐거운
wait in line 줄을 서서 기다리다   enter[éntər] 동 들어가다   up close 바로 가까이에
field[fi:ld] 몡 밭   plant[plænt] 몡 식물   design[dizáin] 몡 디자인 동 설계하다
giant[dʒáiənt] 쥉 거대한   pumpkin[pʌ́mpkin] 몡 호박   get lost 길을 잃다
reach[ri:tʃ] 동 도달하다   staff[stæf] 몡 직원   explore[iksplɔ́:r] 동 탐험하다
take a bath 목욕하다   grain[grein] 몡 곡물; *낟알   recommend[rèkəménd] 동 추천하다
[문제] adventure[ædvéntʃər] 몡 모험   tourist spot 관광 명소   harvest[há:rvist] 몡 수확
season[sí:zn] 몡 철, 계절   location[loukéiʃən] 몡 위치   prize[praiz] 몡 상, 상품

구문   6행   **It** was amusing [**to see** a lot of people *waiting* in line **to enter**].
• It은 가주어이고, to see 이하가 진주어
• see + 목적어 + v-ing: …가 ~하는 것을 보다
• to enter: '…하기 위해'라는 의미로, 목적을 나타내는 부사적 용법의 to부정사
13행   In the maze, I didn't know **where to go**, even with a map.
• where to-v: 어디로 …할지
13행   The corn was **so** tall **that I couldn't** see anything around me.
• so + 형용사[부사] + that + 주어 + can't ~: 너무 …해서 ~할 수 없다
16행   After exploring the maze, I took a corn bath, **which** *was filled with* corn grains.
• which: a corn bath를 보충 설명하는 계속적 용법의 주격 관계대명사
• be filled with: …으로 가득 차다

STRATEGIC SUMMARY   corn, size, pumpkin, bath

VOCABULARY REVIEW

A **1** map **2** bath **3** recommend **4** season
B **1** c **2** b   C **1** d **2** a **3** b **4** c

VOCABULARY PREVIEW

A **1** b **2** d **3** a **4** c   B **1** dry **2** cause **3** reduce **4** same

★*Foot Odor*

1 d **2** c **3** the bacteria become very active **4** a **5** b

> **Q:** 제 발에서 악취가 나서 저는 당황스럽습니다. 무엇이 그 나쁜 냄새가 나게 하는 건가요? 어떻게 하면 없앨 수 있나요? 저는 도움이 좀 필요합니다.
>
> **A:** 안녕하세요, 저는 Page 박사입니다. 제가 당신의 문제에 도움을 줄 수 있을 것 같습니다. 그 나쁜 냄새는 당신의 발에 있는 작은 박테리아들에 의해 나는 것입니다. 그것들은 당신의 발에 있는 땀을 먹고 나서 노폐물을 만들어냅니다. (사람은 보통 하루에 약 500ml의 땀을 흘립니다.) 이 노폐물이 당신의 발에서 아주 고약한 냄새가 나게 합니다. 당신의 발에서 땀이 많이 날 때, 박테리아는 아주 왕성해지기 때문에 그것은 더 악화됩니다!
> 냄새를 없애기 위해, 당신은 발을 자주 씻어야 합니다. 이것이 땀을 씻어낼 것입니다. 당신은 또한 발, 특히 발가락 사이를 잘 말려야 합니다. 이는 박테리아가 <u>눅눅한 장소를 매우 좋아하기 때문입니다</u>. 면으로 만든 양말을 신는 것이 발을 건조하게 유지하는 데 도움이 됩니다. 그리고 당신은 신발을 건조하게 유지하고 매일 같은 신발을 신지 않으려고 노력할 필요가 있습니다. 마지막으로, 약간의 식초를 섞은 따뜻한 물에 발을 15분간 담그세요. 식초가 박테리아를 죽이고 냄새를 줄여줍니다.

어휘   odor[óudər] 명 냄새, 악취   embarrassed[imbǽrəst] 형 당황스러운   stinky[stíŋki] 형 악취가 나는
cause[kɔːz] 동 …을 야기하다 명 원인   get rid of …을 제거하다   bacteria[bæktíəriə]
명 *(pl.)* 박테리아, 세균   sweat[swet] 명 땀 동 땀을 흘리다   produce[prədjúːs] 동 생산하다
waste[weist] 명 낭비; *폐기물   active[ǽktiv] 형 활동적인   dry[drai] 동 말리다 형 마른
toe[tou] 명 발가락   cotton[kátn] 명 면직물   same[seim] 형 같은, 동일한   soak[souk] 동 담그다
mix[miks] 동 섞다, 혼합하다   vinegar[vínəgər] 명 식초   reduce[ridjúːs] 동 줄이다
[문제] avoid[əvɔ́id] 동 방지하다, 피하다   disease[dizíːz] 명 질병   solution[səlúːʃən] 명 해결법
smelly[sméli] 형 냄새 나는   damp[dæmp] 형 축축한, 습기 찬   as … as possible 가능한 한 …하게

구문   8행   This waste **makes** your feet very **stinky**.
• make + 목적어 + 형용사: …가 ~하게 하다

11행   **To get rid of** the smell, you should wash your feet often.
• To get rid of: '…하기 위해'라는 의미로, 목적을 나타내는 부사적 용법의 to부정사구

14행   [**Wearing** socks *made of cotton*] **helps** your feet **stay** dry.
• Wearing 이하의 문장의 주어로 쓰인 동명사구로, 단수 취급함
• made of cotton은 socks를 수식하는 과거분사구
• help + 목적어 + 동사원형: …가 ~하는 것을 돕다

15행   And you need to **keep** your shoes **dry** and try *not to wear* the same shoes every day.
• keep + 목적어 + 형용사: …을 ~한 상태로 유지하다
• not to-v: to부정사의 부정은 to부정사 앞에 not을 붙임

STRATEGIC ORGANIZER   sweat, waste, get rid of, change, vinegar

VOCABULARY REVIEW

A **1** waste **2** soak **3** vinegar **4** toe

B **1** d **2** b   C **1** d **2** a **3** b **4** c

unit *03* LITERATURE

pp. 17-20

VOCABULARY PREVIEW

A **1** b **2** c **3** a **4** d   B **1** stay **2** wrong **3** accept **4** scold

My Sweet Orange Tree

1 c **2** He wanted her to put them in the empty vase on her desk. **3** c **4** b **5** d

---

어느 날, 선생님이 Zeze에게 방과 후에 남으라고 말한다. 선생님은 그가 누군가의 정원에서 약간의 꽃을 훔쳐와서 자신에게 주었기 때문에 그를 야단친다.

선생님: Zeze, 왜 이 꽃을 훔쳤니? 도둑질이 나쁘다는 걸 모르니?
Zeze: 저는 선생님께 꽃을 드리고 싶었어요. 그렇지만 저는 돈이나 정원이 없어요.
선생님: 하지만 왜?
Zeze: 그러면 선생님 책상 위에 있는 빈 꽃병에 꽃을 꽂으실 수 있잖아요. 선생님은 간식 살 돈을 저에게 주시는 것 같이 항상 저에게 잘 해주시잖아요.
선생님: 네가 필요하면 나는 너에게 간식비를 매일 줄 수도 있단다.
Zeze: 저는 그것을 매일 받을 수 없어요. Dorotilia처럼 저보다 더 가난한 다른 학생들이 있어요. 그 애에게는 열 명의 형제자매들이 있고, 그녀의 어머니는 돈을 벌기 위해 세탁을 해야 해요. 제 어머니는 저에게 늘 더 가난한 사람들과 나누라고 가르치셨어요.
선생님: (Zeze의 어깨에 손을 올리며) 알았다. 하지만 누군가 너에게 주는 게 아니라면 더는 꽃을 나에게 가져오지 마라. 알겠지?
Zeze: 알겠어요, 약속할게요. 하지만 선생님의 꽃병은 항상 비어 있겠죠?
선생님: 아니, 절대 비어 있지 않을 거야. 내가 그것을 볼 때, 나는 항상 세상에서 가장 아름다운 꽃들을 보게 될 거야. 그리고 나의 최고의 제자가 나에게 그 꽃들을 주었다고 생각할 거야.

어휘   stay[stei] 동 계속 머무르다, 남다   scold[skould] 동 야단치다   steal[sti:l] 동 훔치다
garden[gá:rdn] 명 뜰, 정원   wrong[rɔ:ŋ] 형 틀린; *나쁜   empty[émpti] 형 비어 있는
vase[veis] 명 꽃병   snack[snæk] 명 간식   accept[æksépt] 동 받아들이다   laundry[lɔ́:ndri]
명 세탁물; *세탁(일)   earn[əːrn] 동 (돈을) 벌다   share[ʃɛər] 동 나누다   bring[briŋ] 동 가져오다
unless[ənlés] 접 …하지 않는 한   promise[prámis] 동 약속하다   [문제] shy[ʃai] 형 부끄러워하는
expensive[ikspénsiv] 형 비싼   brave[breiv] 형 용감한   playful[pléifl] 형 장난기 많은
cheerful[tʃíərfəl] 형 발랄한   warm-hearted[wɔ́:rmhà:rtid] 형 마음이 따뜻한

구문   1행   One day, the teacher **asks** Zeze **to stay** after class.
　　　　　• ask + 목적어 + to-v: …에게 ~을 요청하다
　　　5행   I wanted to **give you flowers**.
　　　　　• give + 간접목적어 + 직접목적어: …에게 ~을 주다
　　　14행   There are other students [**who** are poorer than me, like Dorotilia].
　　　　　• who 이하는 other students를 수식하는 주격 관계대명사절
　　　22행   When I look at it, I'll always see **the most beautiful flowers in** the world.
　　　　　• the + 최상급 + in …: …에서 가장 ~한

4

VOCABULARY REVIEW

A **1** bring **2** promised **3** laundry **4** unless
B **1** d **2** b C **1** c **2** a **3** d **4** c

unit 04 PSYCHOLOGY

pp. 21-24

VOCABULARY PREVIEW

A **1** c **2** d **3** b **4** a B **1** recover **2** silent **3** allow **4** turn off

★The Reactance Theory

1 d **2** b **3** We feel like doing the opposite to recover our lost freedom. **4** c **5** c

> 선생님께서 당신에게 수업 중에 스마트폰을 끄라고 하신다고 상상해보라. 당신은 무엇을 하고 싶은가? 당신은 그것을 더 많이 사용하고 싶다! 그것은 왜 그럴까? 반발 이론이 그 이유를 설명한다.
>
> 그것은 사람들이 무엇을 할지 결정하는 자유를 가지고 있다고 말한다. 어떤 사람이 당신에게 무엇을 하라고 말하면, 당신은 자유를 잃고 있다는 느낌이 든다. 그래서, 당신은 당신의 잃어버린 자유를 되찾기 위해 그 반대로 행동하고 싶은 기분이 든다. 더구나, 당신의 자유가 더 강하게 제약을 받으면, 당신의 감정은 더 강해진다. 로미오와 줄리엣이 허락받지 못했을 때 서로 얼마나 깊이 사랑했는지 생각해보라!
>
> 많은 기업들이 사람들이 그들의 제품을 더 많이 원하도록 하기 위해 이 이론을 이용한다. 예를 들어, 그들은 종종 '한정판' 또는 '단 하루만 할인'과 같은 표현들을 사용한다. 그들은 고객들이 원하는 때 언제든지 그들의 제품을 구매할 수 있는 자유를 제한한다. 그러면 고객들은 할인이 끝나기 전에 그 제품들을 사야 한다고 느낀다.
>
> 그러니, 당신의 남동생이 잠깐 조용히 해야 할 필요가 있다면, "조용히 해!"라고 소리 지르지 마라.

어휘
imagine[imǽdʒin] 동 상상하다 turn off …을 끄다 reactance[riǽktəns] 명 반발, 저항
theory[θíːəri] 명 이론 explain[ikspléin] 동 설명하다 reason[ríːzn] 명 이유 freedom[fríːdəm]
명 자유 opposite[ápəzit] 명 정반대의 일 recover[rikʌ́vər] 동 되찾다, 회복하다
restricted[ristríktid] 형 제한된, 제약을 받는 allow[əláu] 동 허락하다, 용납하다 limited[límitid]
형 한정된 (limit 동 제한하다) edition[idíʃən] 명 (출판물 등의) 판 sale[seil] 명 판매; *세일, 할인 판매
customer[kʌ́stəmər] 명 손님, 고객 product[prádʌkt] 명 상품, 제품 silent[sáilənt] 형 조용한
yell[jel] 동 소리치다 [문제] attract[ətrǽkt] 동 끌어들이다 background[bǽkgràund] 명 배경
describe[diskráib] 동 서술하다, 묘사하다 real-life[ríːəllàif] 형 실제의, 현실의 prove[pruːv]
동 증명하다 respect[rispékt] 명 존경, 존중 press[pres] 동 누르다

구문
1행 Imagine that your teacher **tells** you **to turn off** your smartphone during class.
  • tell + 목적어 + to-v: …에게 ~하라고 말하다

6행 It says that people have the freedom **to decide** *what to do*.
  • to decide: the freedom을 수식하는 형용사적 용법의 to부정사
  • what to-v: '무엇을 …할지'라는 의미로, 동사 decide의 목적어 역할을 함

10행 So, you **feel like doing** the opposite *to recover* your lost freedom.
  • feel like v-ing: …을 하고 싶다
  • to recover: '…하기 위해'라는 의미로, 목적을 나타내는 부사적 용법의 to부정사

13행 Think about [**how** deeply Romeo and Juliet loved each other] when they weren't *allowed to* (love each other)!

5

- how 이하는 '의문사 + 주어 + 동사' 어순의 간접의문문으로, 전치사 about의 목적어 역할을 함
- allowed to 뒤에 반복되는 부분인 love each other가 생략되어 있음

18행 They limit customers' freedom to buy their products any time [(when) **they want**].
- they want 앞에 any time을 선행사로 하는 관계부사가 생략되어 있음

STRATEGIC SUMMARY decide, lost, recover, limiting

VOCABULARY REVIEW

A **1** lose **2** decide **3** product **4** expression
B **1** d **2** b   C **1** c **2** d **3** d **4** c

unit
05 ART

pp. 25-28

VOCABULARY PREVIEW

A **1** b **2** c **3** d **4** a   B **1** suddenly **2** silly **3** male **4** comedy

★ *The Trocks*

1 a **2** d **3** b **4** well-trained ballet dancers show excellent ballet technique while they act silly
5 c

> 발레에서 무용수들이 사랑스러운 드레스를 입고 화장을 한 채로 무대에 오른다. 하지만 이 발레에는 무언가 이상한 것이 있다. 무용수들이 전부 남자다! 그것은 세계적으로 유명한 남성 발레단인 '몬테카를로 트로카데로 발레단(트록스)'의 공연이다.
>
> 트록스 발레단은 1974년 뉴욕에서 시작되었으며 그들의 <u>장난기 많은</u> 공연으로 유명하다. 남성 무용수들이 모든 여성 역할을 한다. 발레 스커트를 입고 발끝으로 춤을 추는 덩치 큰 남자들을 상상해보라. 그것은 아주 재미있다! 게다가 그들은 진지한 고전 발레 이야기를 희극으로 바꾼다. 예를 들어, <u>빈사의 백조에서 백조는 우아하게 죽어야 한다.</u> 그러나 그들의 버전에서는 백조가 만화 캐릭터처럼 갑자기 죽는다. 게다가 무용수들은 공연을 더 웃기게 하려고 실수를 한다. 예를 들어, 그들은 청중들이 웃을 수 있게 때때로 무대에서 떨어지기도 한다.
>
> 유머 외에도, 트록스 발레단은 훈련이 잘된 발레 무용수들로 유명하다. 그들은 우스꽝스럽게 연기하는 동안 훌륭한 발레 기량을 선보인다. 그래서 그 공연은 발레 팬과 희극 팬 모두의 관심을 동시에 끈다.

어휘   make-up[méikÀp] 몡 화장   performance[pərfɔ́:rməns] 몡 공연   male[meil] 혱 남자의
        play[plei] 동 놀다; *(연극·영화에서) 배역을 맡다   female[fí:meil] 혱 여자의   toe[tou] 몡 발가락;
        *발끝   in addition 게다가   serious[síəriəs] 혱 진지한   classical[klǽsikəl] 혱 고전적인
        comedy[kámədi] 몡 희극, 코미디   version[vɔ́:rʒən] 몡 (이전 것과 약간 다른) 판   suddenly[sÁdnli]
        훈 갑자기   cartoon[ka:rtú:n] 몡 만화   character[kǽriktər] 몡 등장인물   fall off …에서 떨어지다
        audience[ɔ́:diəns] 몡 청중   besides[bisáidz] 전 … 외에   excellent[éksələnt] 혱 훌륭한
        technique[tekní:k] 몡 기량, 기법   act[ækt] 동 행동하다; *연기하다   silly[síli] 혱 어리석은;
        *우스꽝스러운   appeal[əpí:l] 동 관심을 끌다, 매력적이다   [문제] role[roul] 몡 역할
        costume[kástju:m] 몡 의상   playful[pléifl] 혱 장난기 많은   gracefully[gréisfəli] 훈 우아하게
        skillful[skílfəl] 혱 숙련된, 솜씨 좋은

구문   1행   At a ballet, the dancers come onto the stage [**wearing** lovely dresses and make-up].
            - wearing 이하는 동시동작을 나타내는 분사구문

12행 Imagine big men [**wearing** ballet skirts] and [**dancing** on their toes].
  · wearing 이하와 dancing 이하는 big men을 수식하는 현재분사구

17행 What's more, the dancers make some mistakes **to make** their performance *funnier*.
  · to make: '…하기 위해'라는 의미로, 목적을 나타내는 부사적 용법의 to부정사
  · make + 목적어 + 형용사: …을 ～하게 하다

22행 So the performances appeal to **both** fans of ballet **and** fans of comedy ....
  · both A and B: A와 B 둘 다

STRATEGIC ORGANIZER Male, funnier, High, technique

VOCABULARY REVIEW

A **1** performance **2** humor **3** fan **4** audience
B **1** b **2** d   C **1** c **2** a **3** c **4** d

unit 06 SPORTS
pp. 29-32

VOCABULARY PREVIEW

A **1** d **2** c **3** b **4** a   B **1** strict **2** steep **3** miss **4** meet

★The Boston Marathon

1 b **2** b **3** it comes after they are almost out of energy **4** c **5** a

---

보스턴에서 4월의 세 번째 월요일은 애국 기념일이다. 그날은 또한 '마라톤 월요일'이라고도 불린다!

보스턴 마라톤은 1897년에 단 18명의 주자가 참가한 지역 행사로 시작되었다. 현재 그것은 세계에서 가장 오래되고 가장 큰 연례 마라톤이다. 매년, 세계 각지에서 온 3만여 명의 주자가 이 경주에서 달린다.

그 경주는 주자들에게 인기 있을 뿐 아니라 아주 도전적이기도 하다. 보통, 마라톤에는 모든 사람이 참여할 수 있다. 하지만 보스턴 마라톤에서 주자들은 제한 시간 기준을 충족해야 한다. 예를 들어, 20세의 남자 주자는 3시간 5분 이하의 마라톤 기록을 보유해야 한다. 그 기준들은 너무 엄격해서 주자들은 단 1초 차이로 자격을 놓칠 수 있다. 또한 보스턴 마라톤의 코스에는 Heartbreak Hill이라고 불리는 오르막길이 있다. 이 언덕은 특별히 가파르거나 길지는 않지만, 주자들에게는 큰 도전이다. 이는 그것이 그들이 에너지가 거의 다 떨어진 다음에 나오기 때문이다.

이것의 도전적인 특성에도 불구하고, 보스턴 마라톤은 많은 사람들의 사랑을 받는다. 50만 명의 군중들이 이 경기에서 응원한다. 직접 보스턴 마라톤을 보고 즐기는 것이 어떤가?

어휘 patriot[péitriət] 몡 애국자   local[lóukəl] 혱 지역의   annual[ǽnjuəl] 혱 매년의, 연례의
race[reis] 몡 경주   challenging[tʃǽlindʒin] 혱 도전적인 (challenge 몡 도전)   hold[hould] 동 잡고 있다; *(기록 등을) 보유하다   record[rékərd] 몡 기록   standard[stǽndərd] 몡 수준, 기준
strict[strikt] 혱 엄격한, 엄한   miss[mis] 동 놓치다   qualify[kwɑ́ləfài] 동 자격을 얻다
uphill[ʌ́phíl] 혱 오르막의   particularly[pərtíkjulərli] 뷔 특히, 특별히   steep[stiːp] 혱 가파른, 비탈진
nature[néitʃər] 몡 자연; *본질, 특성   crowd[kraud] 몡 군중, 사람들   [문제] train[trein] 동 훈련하다
meet[miːt] 동 만나다; *(필요 등을) 충족시키다

구문 13행 The race is **not only** popular **but also** very challenging for the runners.
  · not only A but also B: A뿐만 아니라 B도

16행 The standards are **so** strict **that** the runners can miss qualifying by just a second.
  · so ... that ~: 너무 …해서 ～하다

17행   Also, the Boston Marathon has an uphill road [**called** Heartbreak Hill] on its course.

- called 이하는 an uphill road를 수식하는 과거분사구

22행   **Why not watch** and **enjoy** the Boston Marathon *for yourself*?

- why not + 동사원형: …하는 게 어때
- for oneself: 스스로

STRATEGIC ORGANIZER   took part, international, strict, energy

VOCABULARY REVIEW

A   **1** annual   **2** patriot   **3** crowd   **4** course
B   **1** b   **2** b   C   **1** b   **2** c   **3** c   **4** a

07 MEDIA

pp. 33-36

VOCABULARY PREVIEW

A   **1** a   **2** d   **3** b   **4** c   B   **1** simple   **2** secretly   **3** show up   **4** reward

★Easter Eggs

1 b   **2** d   **3** We can find one by pressing certain keys at once or clicking the mouse a certain way.   **4** c   **5** a

어느 날 인터넷에서 정보를 찾고 있을 때, 당신은 어떤 단어를 입력하고 '검색'을 클릭한다. 그러면, 작은 컴퓨터 게임이 당신의 브라우저에 나타난다. 이것은 오류가 아니다. 이것은 'Easter egg'이다.

Easter egg는 간단한 메시지, 이미지 혹은 게임과 같이 컴퓨터 프로그램 안에 숨겨진 일종의 내용물이다. Easter egg는 동시에 특정한 키들을 누르거나 일정한 방식으로 마우스를 클릭함으로써 예기치 않게 발견될 수 있다. 'Easter egg'라는 이름은 아이들이 찾을 달걀을 숨겨 놓는 부활절 전통에서 유래한다. 비슷하게, 프로그래머들은 몰래 자신들의 제품에 Easter egg를 넣어둔다. 하지만 이러한 종류의 Easter egg는 컴퓨터 프로그램에서만 발견되는 것은 아니다. DVD에도 숨겨진 볼거리들이 많이 있다. 예를 들어, 당신은 삭제된 장면들이나 배우들과의 인터뷰를 찾아볼 수 있다.

그러면 왜 프로그래머들은 Easter egg를 만들고 숨겨 놓는가? 그들은 사람들이 예상치 못한 것을 찾는 것을 좋아하기 때문에 그렇게 한다. 어떤 사람들은 단지 이 숨겨진 보상을 찾기 위해 DVD나 컴퓨터 프로그램에 있는 메뉴를 확인한다!

어휘   search for …을 찾다   information[infərméiʃən] 명 정보   certain[sə́:rtn] 형 어떤; 일정한
show up 나타나다   error[érər] 명 실수, 오류   hidden[hídn] 형 숨겨진 (hide 동 감추다, 숨기다)
content[kántent] 명 내용물   simple[símpl] 형 간단한, 단순한   unexpectedly[ʌ̀nikspéktidli]
부 예기치 않게   press[pres] 동 누르다   at once 동시에   tradition[trədíʃən] 명 전통
secretly[síːkrətli] 부 몰래   product[prádʌkt] 명 제품   delete[dilíːt] 동 삭제하다
scene[siːn] 명 장면   surprise[sərpráiz] 명 뜻밖의 일   reward[riwɔ́ːrd] 명 보상
[문제] hide-and-seek[hàidnsíːk] 명 숨바꼭질   behind-the-scenes[biháindðəsíːnz] 형 비밀의; *무대
뒤의   origin[ɔ́ːrədʒin] 명 기원   feature[fíːtʃər] 명 특징; *볼거리   interest[íntərəst] 동 관심을 끌다
annoyed[ənɔ́id] 형 짜증이 난   unnecessary[ʌ̀nnésəseri] 형 불필요한

구문   6행   Easter eggs **can be found** unexpectedly *by pressing* certain keys at once or *clicking* the mouse a certain way.

- can be found: '…될 수 있다'라는 의미로, 조동사와 함께 쓰인 수동태
  - by v-ing: …함으로써

9행 The name "Easter egg" comes from the Easter tradition of hiding eggs **for children** *to find*.
  - for children: to부정사의 의미상 주어
  - to find: eggs를 수식하는 형용사적 용법의 to부정사

STRATEGIC SUMMARY hidden, pressing, scenes, finding

VOCABULARY REVIEW

A **1** scene **2** pressed **3** hide **4** errors
B **1** c **2** b   C **1** c **2** d **3** b **4** d

★unit★ 08 ORIGINS
pp. 37-40

VOCABULARY PREVIEW

A **1** b **2** c **3** a **4** d   B **1** tiny **2** melt **3** regular **4** famous

★Chocolate Chip Cookies

1 a **2** b **3** c **4** Ruth used the company's chocolate to make the cookies, and many people followed her recipe **5** d

> 모든 사람들이 초콜릿 칩 쿠키를 매우 좋아한다. 이 인기 있는 쿠키는 1933년에 보스턴의 Ruth Wakefield라는 이름의 한 여성에 의해 만들어졌다.
>
> 어느 날, Ruth는 Toll House Inn이라는 그녀의 식당에 필요한 쿠키를 굽고 있었다. 녹는 초콜릿이 다 떨어졌기 때문에, 그녀는 대신 보통 초콜릿을 사용했다. 그녀는 조각들이 오븐에서 녹기를 기대하면서 그것을 작은 조각들로 쪼갰다. (쿠키는 대개 10분에서 15분 동안 구워진다.) 놀랍게도 초콜릿은 녹지 않았다. 그 결과물은 부드러운 초콜릿 칩이 들어간 달콤하고 맛있는 쿠키였다! 사람들이 그것을 정말 많이 좋아해서 그녀의 조리법은 보스턴의 한 신문에 실리기까지 했다.
>
> 그러는 동안, 식품 회사인 Nestle가 보스턴에서 자신들의 초콜릿 판매가 크게 증가한 것을 알아차렸다. 그것은 Ruth가 쿠키를 만들기 위해 그 회사의 초콜릿을 사용하였고, 많은 사람들이 그녀의 조리법을 따라 했기 때문이다. 그래서 Nestle는 그 조리법을 사서 그들의 초콜릿 포장지에 그것을 게재했다. 곧 초콜릿 칩 쿠키는 전국적으로 유명해졌다. 오늘날, 초콜릿 칩 쿠키는 미국에서 여전히 때때로 Toll House 쿠키라고 불린다.

어휘   bake[beik] 동 굽다   run out of …을 다 써버리다   melt[melt] 동 녹다   regular[régjulər] 형 규칙적인; *보통의   tiny[táini] 형 아주 작은   piece[pi:s] 명 조각   expect[ikspékt] 동 기대하다   result[rizʌ́lt] 명 결과   soften[sɔ́:fən] 동 부드럽게 하다   recipe[résəpi] 명 조리법   print[print] 동 인쇄하다; *게재하다   meanwhile[mí:nwàil] 부 그 동안에   realize[rí:əlàiz] 동 깨닫다, 알아차리다   increase[inkrí:s] 동 증가하다   follow[fálou] 동 (지시 등을) 따르다   packaging[pǽkidʒiŋ] 명 포장지   famous[féiməs] 형 유명한   [문제] by chance 우연히   offer[ɔ́:fər] 동 제공하다   react[riǽkt] 동 반응하다

구문   1행   These popular cookies were created by a woman [**named** Ruth Wakefield] in Boston in 1933.
  - named 이하는 a woman을 수식하는 과거분사구

6행 She cut it into tiny pieces [*expecting* them *to melt* in the oven].

- expecting 이하는 동시동작을 나타내는 분사구문
- expect + 목적어 + to-v: …가 ~하기를 기대하다

8행 **To Ruth's surprise**, the chocolate didn't melt.

- to one's surprise: 놀랍게도

9행 People loved it **so** much **that** her recipe was even printed in a Boston newspaper.

- so … that ~: 너무 …해서 ~하다

STRATEGIC SUMMARY restaurant, melting, recipe, popular

VOCABULARY REVIEW

A *1* soften *2* recipe *3* printed *4* surprise
B *1* c *2* a   C *1* b *2* c *3* a *4* d

★unit★ 09 ECONOMY
pp. 41-44

VOCABULARY PREVIEW

A *1* d *2* a *3* b *4* c   B *1* messy *2* success *3* weakness *4* cheap

★The Hans Brinker Hotel

1 c *2* c *3* c *4* They become curious about the hotel and want to stay there. *5* c

> 많은 회사들이 고객들에게 멋져 보이기를 원한다. 그래서 그들은 그들의 상품의 장점들만을 보여주려고 노력한다. 그러나 네덜란드의 한 호텔은 다르다. 그것은 그것의 약점을 솔직하게 보여주는 것으로 사람들의 관심을 받는다.
>
> Hans Brinker 호텔은 여행자들을 위한 저렴하고 위치 좋은 호텔이다. 그것은 침대가 딸린 방을 제공할 뿐 특별한 것은 없다. 그러나 호텔의 경영자들은 그것이 저렴하다거나 좋은 위치에 있다고 이야기함으로써 호텔을 홍보하지 않는다. 그 대신에, 그들은 호텔의 모든 나쁜 점에 초점을 맞춘다. 그들은 호텔의 열악한 시설과 서비스를 자랑스럽게 광고한다. 광고에는 부러진 의자, 이가 빠진 포크, 그리고 지저분한 침대가 보여진다. 그리고 그들은 또한 "더 이상 나빠질 수 없지만, 저희는 최선을 다하겠습니다."라고 말한다. 결과가 어떨까? 많은 젊은 여행자들이 그 호텔에 대해 궁금해하고 거기에 머물고 싶어한다. 이제, 그곳은 네덜란드에서 가장 인기 있는 호텔들 중 하나이다!
>
> 자, 당신은 사람들의 관심을 끌고 성공하고 싶은가? 그렇다면 남들과 다르게 생각하고 새로운 것을 시도하라. 이것이 성공의 열쇠가 될 수 있다.

어휘 attractive[ətrǽktiv] 형 멋진, 매력적인 advantage[ædvǽntidʒ] 명 장점 attention[əténʃən] 명 관심, 주목 cheap[tʃiːp] 형 (값이) 싼 traveler[trǽvələr] 명 여행자 provide[prəváid] 동 제공하다 promote[prəmóut] 동 홍보하다 location[loukéiʃən] 명 위치 focus on …에 집중하다 proudly[práudli] 부 자랑스럽게 advertise[ǽdvərtàiz] 동 광고하다 (ad 명 광고 (= advertisement)) facility[fəsíləti] 명 (pl.) 시설 chip[tʃip] 동 (컵 등의) 이가 빠지다 messy[mési] 형 지저분한 curious[kjúəriəs] 형 궁금한, 호기심이 많은 successful[səksésfəl] 형 성공한 (success 명 성공) [문제] unique[juːníːk] 형 유일한; *독특한 honestly[ánistli] 부 솔직하게 weakness[wíːknis] 명 약점 describe[diskráib] 동 묘사하다 popularity[pàpjulǽrəti] 명 인기 lead to …로 이어지다

구문 1행 Many companies want to **look attractive** to customers.

- look + 형용사: …하게 보이다

3행 It gets people's attention **by** honestly **showing** its weaknesses.
• by v-ing: …함으로써

11행 Now, it is **one of the most popular hotels** in the Netherlands!
• one of the + 최상급 + 복수명사: 가장 …한 것들 중 하나

14행 This can be **a key to success**.
• a key to + 명사: …의 열쇠

STRATEGIC SUMMARY nice, problems, curious, well-known

VOCABULARY REVIEW

A *1* traveler *2* focus *3* result *4* facility
B *1* c *2* a   C *1* d *2* d *3* c *4* b

unit
10 JOBS

pp. 45-48

VOCABULARY PREVIEW

A *1* b *2* d *3* c *4* a   B *1* real *2* complete *3* create *4* add

★An Interview with a Foley Artist

1 c *2* b *3* c *4* they are usually set up to record the actors' words *5* b

영화를 만드는 데 역할을 맡아 하는 사람은 배우와 감독만이 아닙니다. 효과음 기술자를 포함하여 뒤에서 다른 일들을 하는 사람들이 있습니다. 할리우드의 효과음 기술자인 Amy Parker 씨가 여기에 나와 계십니다.

Q: 효과음 기술자들은 무슨 일을 합니까?
A: 우리의 일은 영화에 쓸 음향 효과를 만드는 것입니다. 우리는 발자국 소리나 문 여는 소리와 같이 우리가 일상생활에서 종종 놓치는 소리들을 만들어냅니다. 우리는 이 세상에 존재하지 않는 소리까지도 만듭니다. 예를 들어, 우리는 *스타워즈*와 같은 공상과학 영화의 광선검 소리를 만듭니다. 이 음향 효과들은 영화를 더 사실적으로 보이게 합니다.

Q: 그렇군요. 하지만 실제 소리에 대해서는 감독들이 영화를 만드는 동안 그것들을 그냥 녹음하지 않나요?
A: 그렇지는 않습니다. 마이크는 보통 배우들의 말을 녹음하기 위해 설치되기 때문에, 그것들은 다른 소리들을 잘 잡아낼 수 없습니다. 그래서 그들은 영화 촬영을 마친 후에 그 소리들을 더하기 위해 우리를 필요로 합니다.

Q: 당신들은 어떻게 일을 하나요?
A: 우리는 큰 화면이 있는 스튜디오에서 일합니다. 영화가 화면에 상영되는 동안, 우리는 동작의 시간에 맞추어가며 음향 효과를 추가합니다. 우리는 흥미로운 물건들을 이용해서 소리를 만들어냅니다. 우리가 주먹으로 치는 소리를 어떻게 만드는지 아세요? 우리는 수박을 칩니다!

어휘 director[diréktər] 명 감독   play a part 역할을 하다   film[film] 명 영화 동 촬영하다
behind the scenes 무대 뒤에서; *막후에서   including[inklúːdiŋ] 전 …을 포함하여   foley[fóuli]
명 효과음 녹음   create[kriéit] 동 창조하다   sound effect 음향 효과   daily life 일상생활
footstep[fútstèp] 명 발자국   sword[sɔːrd] 명 칼, 검   real[ríːəl] 형 진짜의, 현실의
record[rikɔ́ːrd] 동 녹음하다   microphone[máikrəfòun] 명 마이크   set up 설치하다
pick up 집어 올리다; *(신호 · 소리 등을) 포착하다   add[æd] 동 더하다   complete[kəmplíːt]
동 끝마치다   studio[stjúːdiòu] 명 스튜디오, 녹음실   match[mætʃ] 동 어울리다; *맞추다

timing[táimiŋ] 명 타이밍, 특정한 시기   action[ǽkʃən] 명 동작, 움직임   object[ábdʒikt] 명 물건, 사물   punch[pʌntʃ] 동 주먹으로 치다   [문제] professional[prəféʃənl] 형 전문적인   exist[igzíst] 동 존재하다   crash[kræʃ] 동 충돌하다   tool[tu:l] 명 도구

구문   1행   **It's not** just actors and directors **who** play a part in making films.
- It is not … who ~: '~한 것은 …가 아니다'의 의미로, just actors and directors를 강조하는 강조구문

5행   We create sounds [**that** we often miss in our daily lives], ….
- that 이하는 sounds를 수식하는 목적격 관계대명사절

12행   Because the microphones are usually set up **to record** the actors' words, ….
- to record: '…하기 위해'라는 의미로, 목적을 나타내는 부사적 용법의 to부정사

17행   …, we add sound effects, [**matching** the timing of the action].
- matching 이하는 동시동작을 나타내는 분사구문

STRATEGIC SUMMARY   sound effects, non-existing, microphones, match

VOCABULARY REVIEW

A   **1** film   **2** studio   **3** actual   **4** timing
B   **1** c   **2** b   C   **1** b   **2** a   **3** c   **4** d

unit 11 FESTIVALS
pp. 49-52

VOCABULARY PREVIEW

A   **1** c   **2** a   **3** b   **4** d   B   **1** explosive   **2** thrilling   **3** throw   **4** behind

★ *The Festival of San Fermin*

1 d   **2** c   **3** b   **4** it only takes three minutes   **5** b

> San Fermin 축제에 대해 들어본 적 있는가? 그것은 매년 스페인 Pamplona에서 7월 6일부터 14일까지 열린다. 이 축제는 Pamplona 최초의 주교인 성 Fermin을 기리기 위해 시작되었다. 나는 지난 7월 그 축제에 참여했다. 그곳에서 내가 겪은 아주 흥미로운 경험에 대해 이야기하겠다!
>
> 축제는 정오에 폭죽을 쏘는 것으로 시작되었다. '빵'하는 큰 폭발 소리에 참가자들은 서로에게 와인을 뿌리기 시작했다. 물론 나는 다 젖었지만 정말 재미있었다.
>
> 축제 동안에 나는 퍼레이드와 콘서트, 플라멩코 춤과 불꽃놀이를 보았다. 하지만 가장 재미있었던 부분은 황소들의 달리기였다. 여섯 마리의 황소가 투우 경기장까지 825미터의 길을 달리도록 되어 있다. 수백 명의 사람들이 그것들과 함께 달린다. 달리기는 겨우 3분이 걸리기 때문에, 나는 그것이 식은 죽 먹기일 것이라고 생각했다. 하지만 내 바로 뒤에 큰 황소를 보자 나는 무서워졌다. 그래서 나는 최대한 빠르게 달렸다. 이것은 내 인생에서 가장 흥미진진한 경험이었다!

어휘   hold[hould] 동 잡고 있다; *개최하다   honor[ánər] 동 존경하다; *기리다   bishop[bíʃəp] 명 주교   take part in …에 참여하다   fascinating[fǽsənèitiŋ] 형 대단히 흥미로운   experience[ikspíəriəns] 명 경험   fire[faiər] 동 발사(발포)하다   rocket[rákit] 명 로켓; *폭죽   explosive[iksplóusiv] 형 폭발의; *(소리가) 폭탄이 터지는 것 같은   participant[pa:rtísəpənt] 명 참가자   throw[θrou] 동 던지다   flamenco[fla:méŋkou] 명 플라멩코(격정적인 스페인 춤)   firework[fáiərwə̀:rk] 명 (pl.) 불꽃놀이   bull[bul] 명 황소   route[ru:t] 명 길   a piece of cake 식은 죽 먹기   scared[skɛərd] 형 무서워하는   behind[biháind] 전 … 뒤에   thrilling[θríliŋ] 형 아주 신나는

구문　3행　The festival was started **to honor** the first Bishop of Pamplona, Saint Fermin.

　　　　• to honor: '…하기 위해'라는 의미로, 목적을 나타내는 부사적 용법의 to부정사

　　12행　Six bulls **are made to run** an 825-meter route to the bullring.

　　　　• be made to-v: '…하도록 되어지다'라는 의미로, 사역동사의 수동태

　　16행　So I ran **as fast as I could.**

　　　　• as + 부사의 원급 + as + 주어 + can: 가능한 한 …하게

STRATEGIC SUMMARY　rocket, threw, bulls, scared

VOCABULARY REVIEW

A　**1** held　**2** participant　**3** took part in　**4** experience

B　**1** b　**2** d　　　C　**1** d　**2** a　**3** c　**4** d

★unit★ 12 SOCIETY

pp. 53-56

VOCABULARY PREVIEW

A　**1** c　**2** b　**3** d　**4** a　　　B　**1** talent　**2** donate　**3** impact　**4** common

★ The Big Issue

1 c　**2** b　**3** c　**4** It has made people think about the issue of homelessness.　**5** b

---

*빅 이슈*를 읽어본 적이 있는가? 그것은 노숙자들에 의해 판매된다는 점을 제외하면, 평범한 길거리 잡지이다.

　*빅 이슈*는 1991년에 두 명의 영국인 사업가에 의해 창간되었다. 그들은 런던의 길거리에 살던 가난한 사람들을 도와주고 싶었다. 그러나 그들은 그들에게 그저 돈을 주지는 않았다. 대신, 그들에게 일하여 돈을 벌 기회를 주었다. 잡지 행상인으로, 그들은 그 잡지 한 부를 1.25파운드에 사서 2.5파운드에 판다.

　그러면, *빅 이슈*는 무엇을 다루는가? 다른 잡지들처럼, 그 기사들은 스타들과의 인터뷰, 영화 평론, 그리고 전 세계적인 사안을 포함한다. 그것을 특별하게 만드는 것은 사람들이 그 잡지를 위해 자신의 재능을 기부한다는 것이다. 작가들과 디자이너들이 그들의 작업에 대해 돈을 받지 않는다. 그리고 데이비드 베컴과 같은 유명인들이 무료로 표지 모델 일을 한다.

　그 제목이 보여주듯이, 그 잡지는 '큰 문제'를 다루고, 그것은 큰 사회적 영향력을 미쳐왔다. 그것은 사람들이 노숙자 문제에 대해 생각하게 만들었다. 그것은 이제 10개국에서 팔리고, 사람들은 그것을 구매함으로써 노숙자들을 돕는다.

어휘　issue[íʃuː] 몡 주제, 쟁점　　common[kámən] 혱 흔한; *평범한　　magazine[mæɡəzíːn] 몡 잡지
except[iksépt] 젭 …라는 점만 제외하면　　homeless[hóumlis] 혱 노숙자의 (homelessness 몡 집 없음, 노숙자임)　　found[faund] 통 설립하다　　offer[ɔ́ːfər] 통 제공하다　　vendor[véndər] 몡 행상인, 노점상　　deal with …을 다루다　　article[áːrtikl] 몡 글, 기사　　include[inklúːd] 통 포함하다
review[rivjúː] 몡 평론, 논평　　global[ɡlóubəl] 혱 세계적인　　donate[dóuneit] 통 기증하다, 기부하다
talent[tǽlənt] 몡 (타고난) 재능　　celebrity[səlébrəti] 몡 유명 인사　　cover[kávər] 몡 덮개; *(책의) 표지　　for free 무료로　　indicate[índikèit] 통 나타내다, 보여주다　　address[ədrés] 통 (문제·상황 등을) 다루다　　social[sóuʃəl] 혱 사회적인　　impact[ímpækt] 몡 영향
[문제] government[ɡávərnmənt] 몡 정부

3행 They wanted to help poor people [**who** were living on the streets of London].
- who 이하는 poor people을 수식하는 주격 관계대명사절

5행 Instead, they **offered them chances** *to make* money by working.
- offer + 간접목적어 + 직접목적어: …에게 ～을 제공하다
- to make: chances를 수식하는 형용사적 용법의 to부정사

9행 **What** *makes* it *special* is that people donate their talents for the magazine.
- What: '…하는 것'의 의미로, 선행사를 포함하는 관계대명사
- make + 목적어 + 형용사: …을 ～하게 하다

17행 It has **made** people **think** about the issue of homelessness.
- 사역동사(make) + 목적어 + 동사원형: …가 ～하게 하다

STRATEGIC ORGANIZER   homeless, magazine, donate, issue

VOCABULARY REVIEW

A   *1* celebrity   *2* found   *3* article   *4* vendor
B   *1* d   *2* b   C   *1* b   *2* c   *3* a   *4* b

---

unit 13 HUMAN BODY   pp. 57-60

VOCABULARY PREVIEW

A   *1* b   *2* a   *3* d   *4* c   B   *1* keep   *2* finish   *3* fill   *4* remember

★The Human Stomach

1 d   *2* c   *3* b   *4* we have to eat more food to fill it   *5* c

---

당신이 방금 식당에서 밥을 많이 먹었다고 상상해보라. 당신은 배가 매우 부르지만, 종업원이 무료로 당신에게 치즈 케이크를 가져다준다. 방금 전에, 당신은 더 이상 먹을 수 없을 것이라고 느꼈다. 하지만 당신은 어쨌든 치즈 케이크를 먹는다!

당신은 이미 배가 불렀는데 어떻게 더 먹을 수 있는가? 사람의 위는 <u>크기가 변하기</u> 때문에 당신은 이렇게 할 수 있는 것이다. 그것은 당신이 얼마나 먹느냐에 따라 더 커지거나 더 작아진다. 대개 사람의 위는 길이가 12인치, 폭은 6인치 정도이며, 1리터의 음식을 담을 수 있다. 하지만 당신이 많이 먹으면, 그것은 풍선처럼 늘어나서 2리터 혹은 그 이상을 담을 수 있다! 그리고 나서, 당신이 다 먹고 나면, 그것은 천천히 더 작아져서 정상적인 크기로 다시 돌아온다.

그러나 당신이 항상 과식을 하면, 당신의 위는 계속 커지게 될 것이다. 그렇게 되면, 당신은 위를 채우기 위해 더 많은 음식을 먹어야 한다. 이는 당신이 과체중이 되게 할 수 있다. 그러므로 당신의 위를 잘 다뤄야 한다는 것을 기억하라. 당신이 더 먹을 수 있다는 사실이 당신이 더 먹어야 한다는 것을 의미하지는 않는다.

어휘   full[ful] 혱 가득 찬; *배부른   stomach[stʌ́mək] 몡 위   depending on …에 따라
hold[hould] 통 잡고 있다; *담다   stretch[stretʃ] 통 늘어나다   finish[fíniʃ] 통 끝나다
return[ritə́ːrn] 통 돌아오다; *(이전 상태로) 되돌아가다   normal[nɔ́ːrməl] 혱 보통의, 정상적인
overeat[òuvəríːt] 통 과식하다   keep[kiːp] 통 …을 계속하다   fill[fil] 통 채우다
overweight[óuvərwèit] 혱 과체중의   remember[rimémbər] 통 기억하다
treat[triːt] 통 다루다, 대하다   mean[miːn] 통 의미하다   [문제] benefit[bénəfit] 몡 이득

구문   1행 Imagine you **have** just **eaten** a large meal at a restaurant.
- have eaten: '(막) …했다'라는 의미로, 완료를 나타내는 현재완료

2행 A moment ago, you felt like you could**n't** eat **anymore**.
  • not … anymore: 더 이상 …않다

9행 Then, after you **finish eating**, it slowly gets smaller and returns to its normal size again.
  • finish는 동명사를 목적어로 취하는 동사

12행 So **remember to treat** your stomach well.
  • remember to-v: (미래에) …할 것을 기억하다

13행 The fact [**that** you can eat more] doesn't mean that you *should* (eat more).
  • that: the fact와 동격인 명사절을 이끄는 접속사
  • should 뒤에 반복되는 부분인 eat more가 생략되어 있음

STRATEGIC SUMMARY full, stretch, returns, overweight

VOCABULARY REVIEW

A *1* overweight *2* mean *3* treats *4* for free
B *1* a *2* d   C *1* c *2* b *3* c *4* a

NATURE

pp. 61-64

VOCABULARY PREVIEW

A *1* d *2* a *3* b *4* c   B *1* risky *2* violent *3* rare *4* professional

Storm Chasing

1 a *2* c *3* They push against each other. *4* c *5* b

폭풍은 아주 위험할 수 있어서, 그것에서 멀리 떨어져 있는 것이 가장 좋습니다. 하지만 폭풍 추격자라고 불리는 어떤 이들은 폭풍을 찾습니다. 전문 폭풍 추격자인 Tom Hale이 폭풍 추격에 대해 우리에게 말해주기 위해 여기에 있습니다.

Q: 폭풍 추격자는 무엇을 합니까?
A: 기본적으로, 우리는 폭풍을 뒤쫓습니다. 그러고 나서, 우리는 그것들을 관찰하고, 기록하고, 사진을 찍습니다. 우리가 왜 이것을 하냐고요? 어떤 이들은 단지 호기심에서 폭풍을 뒤쫓습니다. 저와 같이 많은 다른 이들은 언제 그리고 어떻게 그것들이 형성되는지와 같은 폭풍에 대한 정보를 연구하고 제공하기 위해 그것을 합니다.

Q: 폭풍이 어떻게 형성되는지 설명해주실 수 있습니까?
A: 따뜻하고 습한 공기가 차가운 공기와 만날 때 이러한 다른 두 공기 덩어리가 서로 밀어냅니다. 이것이 폭우, 번개, 그리고 천둥을 동반한 맹렬한 공기의 움직임을 만들어냅니다. 이것이 폭풍이 발생하는 방식입니다.

Q: 폭풍 추격자들은 어떤 종류의 장비를 이용합니까?
A: 우리는 어디에 폭풍이 있는지 찾기 위해 최첨단 장비를 이용합니다. 예를 들어, 위성지도는 우리에게 폭풍이 어디에서 발달하고 있는지를 보여주고, GPS 시스템은 우리가 그 폭풍을 따라가도록 돕습니다. 우리가 폭풍에 가까이 가면, 특별하게 고안된 차량이 외부의 어떤 위험에서도 우리를 보호합니다.

Q: 무엇이 당신을 폭풍 추격에 끌리게 합니까?
A: 폭풍 추격은 위험하게 들릴지도 모릅니다. 하지만 자연의 진기한 아름다움을 포착하는 순간들은 잊을 수 없습니다. 당신이 이러한 놀라운 광경을 보게 되면, 당신도 폭풍을 뒤쫓고 싶어질지도 모릅니다!

어휘　storm[stɔːrm] 명 폭풍　chaser[tʃéisər] 명 추격자 (chase 동 쫓다)　professional[prəféʃənl]
형 전문적인; *전문의, 프로의　mass[mæs] 명 덩어리, 덩이　violent[váiələnt] 형 폭력적인; *격렬한,
맹렬한　lightning[láitniŋ] 명 번개　thunder[θʌ́ndər] 명 천둥　equipment[ikwípmənt] 명 장비
high-tech[hàiték] 형 첨단 기술의　satellite[sǽtəlàit] 명 위성　develop[divéləp] 동 발달하다;
개발하다　GPS(Global Positioning System) 위성 위치 확인 시스템　vehicle[víːikl] 명 차량, 탈것
risky[ríski] 형 위험한　capture[kǽptʃər] 동 포착하다, 담아내다　rare[rɛər] 형 진기한
unforgettable[ʌ̀nfərgétəbl] 형 잊을 수 없는　sight[sait] 명 광경　[문제] unusual[ʌnjúːʒuəl]
형 특이한　predict[pridíkt] 동 예측하다　out of interest 흥미로, 호기심에서　extreme[ikstríːm]
형 극도의　attract[ətrǽkt] 동 마음을 끌다

구문　1행　Storms can be very dangerous, so **it**'s best [**to stay** away from them].
　　　• it은 가주어이고, to stay 이하가 진주어
　　1행　But some people, (who are) **called** storm chasers, look for storms.
　　　• called 앞에 '주격 관계대명사 + be동사'가 생략되어 있음
　　7행　... information about storms, such as [**when** (they form)] and [**how** they form].
　　　• when과 how 이하는 '의문사 + 주어 + 동사' 어순의 간접의문문으로, 전치사구 such as의 목적어
　　　　역할을 함
　　14행　For example, satellite maps **show us where a storm is developing**, and GPS
　　　systems *help* us *follow* the storm.
　　　• show + 간접목적어 + 직접목적어: …에게 ~을 보여주다
　　　• help + 목적어 + 동사원형: …가 ~하도록 돕다
　　20행　If you **happen to see** these wonderful sights, ...
　　　• happen to-v: …하게 되다

STRATEGIC SUMMARY　follow, equipment, protect, capture

VOCABULARY REVIEW

A　**1** satellites　**2** danger　**3** captured　**4** equipment
B　**1** a　**2** d　　　C　**1** c　**2** a　**3** b　**4** d

15 WORLD
pp. 65-68

VOCABULARY PREVIEW

A　**1** d　**2** b　**3** c　**4** a　　B　**1** thin　**2** winner　**3** single　**4** strength

★The Wodaabe Tribe

1 a　**2** beautiful men are more successful at getting girlfriends or wives　**3** b　**4** b　**5** c

> 남자들에게 아름다움과 힘 중 어떤 것이 더 중요할까? 아프리카 중서부의 Wodaabe 부족 남자들에게는 아름다움이다!
> 그것은 아름다운 남자들이 여자 친구나 아내를 얻는 데 더 성공적이기 때문이다. 1년에 한 번, 그들은 Gerewol이라고
> 불리는 축제에서 누가 가장 아름다운지 판단하기 위해 경쟁하기까지 한다.
> 　그렇다면 Wodaabe 부족은 어떤 특징들을 아름답다고 생각할까? 더 밝은 피부색, 얇은 코, 키가 크고 날씬한 몸,
> 그리고 하얀 치아가 모두 필수적이다. 의식에서 남자들은 자신의 얼굴을 노랗고 빨간 가루로 덮고, 코에는 흰색 줄을
> 그린다. 그들은 또한 춤을 추며 입을 크게 벌려 치아를 보여준다.

어휘   beauty[bjúːti] 몡 아름다움   strength[streŋθ] 몡 힘, 기운   tribe[traib] 몡 부족
successful[səksésfəl] 혱 성공적인   compete[kəmpíːt] 통 경쟁하다   feature[fíːtʃər] 몡 특징
consider[kənsídər] 통 여기다, 생각하다   light[lait] 혱 밝은   thin[θin] 혱 얇은, 가는   slim[slim]
혱 날씬한   essential[isénʃəl] 혱 필수적인   ceremony[sérəmòuni] 몡 의식   cover[kʌ́vər] 통
덮다, 가리다   draw[drɔː] 통 그리다   judge[dʒʌdʒ] 몡 판사; *심사위원 통 판단하다   single[síŋgl]
혱 독신의   look[luk] 몡 (pl.) 외모   winner[wínər] 몡 우승자   admire[ædmáiər] 통 존경하다,
칭찬하다   marry[mǽri] 통 결혼하다   [문제] contest[kántest] 몡 대회 (contestant 몡 참가자)
various[vɛ́əriəs] 혱 여러 가지의   decorate[dékərèit] 통 장식하다, 꾸미다

구문   5행   That's because beautiful men are more successful at [**getting** girlfriends or wives].
               • getting 이하는 전치사 at의 목적어 역할을 하는 동명사구
        8행   ..., they even compete in a festival called Gerewol **to see** [*who* is the most
             beautiful].
               • to see: '…하기 위해'라는 의미로, 목적을 나타내는 부사적 용법의 to부정사
               • who 이하는 '의문사(주어) + 동사' 어순의 간접의문문으로, 동사 see의 목적어 역할을 함
       16행   These judges are single Wodaabe women [**who** are chosen for their beauty].
               • who 이하는 single Wodaabe women을 수식하는 주격 관계대명사절
       19행   The winner also has a chance **to marry** the most beautiful woman in the tribe!
               • to marry: a chance를 수식하는 형용사적 용법의 to부정사

STRATEGIC ORGANIZER   compete, standards, prize, marry

VOCABULARY REVIEW

A   **1** light   **2** skin   **3** consider   **4** powder
B   **1** d   **2** b   C   **1** d   **2** a   **3** d   **4** c

unit
16 TRAVEL
                          pp. 69-72

VOCABULARY PREVIEW

A   **1** c   **2** b   **3** d   **4** a   B   **1** imaginary   **2** foreign   **3** protect   **4** fearless

★*The Galapagos Islands*

1 c   **2** it has barely been touched by humans   **3** b   **4** c   **5** c

그러나 이 아름다운 장소를 보호하기 위해 관광객들이 지켜야 하는 몇몇 규칙들이 있다. 야생 동물을 방해하지 마라. 기본적으로 당신은 동물들을 만지거나 먹이를 줄 수 없다. 또한, 타지의 동물들을 데려가서도 안 된다. 그것들은 섬의 생태계에 해를 끼칠 수 있다.

이제 갈라파고스 섬에서 특별한 휴가를 보낼 준비가 되었는가? 그것은 평생에 한 번밖에 없는 경험이 될 것이다!

어휘 enchanted[intʃéntid] 형 마법에 걸린   island[áilənd] 명 섬   imaginary[imǽdʒənèri] 형 상상에만 존재하는   fairy tale 동화   barely[béərli] 부 거의 …않다   unique[juːníːk] 형 독특한   wildlife[wáildlàif] 명 야생 동물   step[step] 동 한 걸음 내디디다   exotic[igzátik] 형 이국적인   face to face 서로 얼굴을 맞대고   booby[búːbi] 명 부비새   lizard[lízərd] 명 도마뱀   run away 도망치다   sea lion 바다사자   protect[prətékt] 동 보호하다   rule[ruːl] 명 규칙   follow[fálou] 동 따라가다; *(지시 등을) 따르다   disturb[distə́ːrb] 동 방해하다   feed[fiːd] 동 먹이를 주다   bring along 데리고 오다   foreign[fɔ́ːrən] 형 외국의, 타지방의   damage[dǽmidʒ] 동 피해를 입히다   once-in-a-lifetime[wʌ́nsinəláiftaim] 형 일생에 한 번의   [문제] discovery[diskʌ́vəri] 명 발견   development[divéləpmənt] 명 개발   fearless[fíərlis] 형 두려움을 모르는

구문 4행 **As** the islands are 1,000 km away from South America, they *have* barely *been touched* by humans.
- as: 이유를 나타내는 접속사
- have been touched: '…되어져 왔다'라는 의미로, 계속을 나타내는 현재완료 수동태

9행 What's more, the animals on these islands **are famous for** [*being* fearless toward humans].
- be famous for: …로 유명하다
- being 이하는 전치사 for의 목적어 역할을 하는 동명사구

12행 …, there are some rules [(which[that]) **tourists** should follow].
- tourist 앞에 some rules를 선행사로 하는 목적격 관계대명사가 생략되어 있음

STRATEGIC SUMMARY natural, afraid, rules, bring

VOCABULARY REVIEW

A *1* barely *2* disturb *3* feed *4* shy
B *1* b *2* c   C *1* b *2* a *3* b *4* d

★*unit* *17* TEENS
pp. 73-76

VOCABULARY PREVIEW

A *1* b *2* d *3* c *4* a   B *1* trust *2* upset *3* private *4* moreover

★*Brian's Problem*
1 d *2* she may think he is hiding something from her *3* c *4* a *5* c

Phil 박사님께,
제 여자친구는 제 이메일과 휴대전화의 비밀번호를 알고 싶어 합니다. 하지만 그것들은 개인적인 것이라 저는 그녀에게

말해주고 싶지 않아요. 제가 어떻게 해야 하죠?

Brian

Brian에게,

당신의 여자친구는 연인이 모든 것을 공유해야 한다고 생각하는지도 모릅니다. 당신이 원하지 않으면, 그녀에게 당신의 비밀번호를 알려줄 필요가 없습니다. 하지만 당신은 그녀에게 당신이 사생활을 원하는 이유를 말해주어야 합니다. 그러지 않으면, 그녀는 당신이 그녀로부터 무언가를 숨기고 있다고 생각할지도 모릅니다.

신뢰는 관계에 있어 매우 중요합니다. 하지만, 사적인 메시지를 읽는 것은 종종 오해를 불러일으킬 수 있습니다. 그리고 이것은 당신들이 서로를 향한 신뢰를 잃게 할 수 있습니다. 게다가, 이것은 단지 당신들 두 사람에게만 영향을 주는 것이 아닙니다. 또한, 당신은 다른 사람들의 사생활을 침해할지도 모릅니다. 예를 들어, 당신에게 보낸 메시지를 당신의 여자친구가 읽는다는 것을 알면 당신의 친구들은 기분 나쁠지도 모릅니다.

그녀에게 당신의 비밀번호를 알려주면, 그녀는 잠깐은 행복할 것입니다. 하지만 나중에, 그것은 당신과 그녀와의, 그리고 당신의 친구들과의 관계를 해칠 수 있습니다. 그러니, 당신은 당신의 이유를 설명할 필요가 있고, 그러면 그녀는 이해할 것입니다. 기억하세요. 정직이 최선의 방책입니다.

Phil 박사

어휘   password[pǽswə̀ːrd] 명 비밀번호   private[práivət] 형 사적인 (privacy 명 사생활)   share[ʃɛər] 동 공유하다   otherwise[ʌ́ðərwàiz] 부 그렇지 않으면   hide[haid] 동 감추다   trust[trʌst] 명 신뢰 동 신뢰하다   relationship[riléiʃənʃip] 명 관계   cause[kɔːz] 동 …을 야기하다   misunderstanding[mìsʌndərstǽndiŋ] 명 오해   moreover[mɔːróuvər] 부 게다가   affect[əfékt] 동 영향을 미치다   upset[ʌ̀psét] 형 속상한, 마음이 상한   hurt[həːrt] 동 다치게 하다, 아프게 하다   honesty[ánisti] 명 정직, 솔직함   policy[páləsi] 명 정책; *방책   [문제] weak point 약점   invade[invéid] 동 침략하다; *(권리 등을) 침해하다

구문   9행   But you should **give her your reasons** for wanting privacy.
- give + 간접목적어 + 직접목적어: …에게 ～을 주다

13행   And this can **make** you **lose** trust towards each other.
- 사역동사(make) + 목적어 + 동사원형: …가 ～하게 하다

15행   For example, your friends may be upset **to know** that your girlfriend reads ….
- to know: 감정의 원인을 나타내는 부사적 용법의 to부정사

STRATEGIC SUMMARY   passwords, share, trust, affect

VOCABULARY REVIEW

A   *1* cause   *2* misunderstanding   *3* explain   *4* password

B   *1* d   *2* a   C   *1* b   *2* d   *3* c   *4* b

unit 18 HISTORY
pp. 77-80

VOCABULARY PREVIEW

A   *1* a   *2* c   *3* d   *4* b   B   *1* name   *2* evidence   *3* nearly   *4* realize

★*Who Discovered America?*

1 d   *2* d   *3* c   *4* he thought he was in eastern India   *5* b

'크리스토퍼 콜럼버스가 1492년에 아메리카 대륙을 발견했다.' 많은 사람들은 이것이 사실이라고 생각한다. 그러나 그가 정말 그랬을까? 어떤 사람들은 이 생각에 동의하지 않는다. 여기 그 근거들이 있다.

첫째로, 콜럼버스보다 더 일찍 아메리카를 발견한 사람들이 있었다. 아메리카 원주민들에 대해 생각해 보라. 그들은 그들의 선조들이 약 12,000년 전에 아시아에서 건너간 이래로 이미 그곳에서 살고 있었다. 둘째로, 콜럼버스는 심지어 아메리카에 도달한 최초의 유럽인도 아니었다. 과학자들은 바이킹들이 아메리카 북부에 있었다는 증거를 찾아냈다. 그들은 이 북유럽 사람들이 콜럼버스보다 거의 오백 년 이전에 아메리카에 왔다고 추정한다. 게다가 콜럼버스가 아메리카에 왔을 때, 그는 심지어 자신이 어디에 있는지조차 몰랐다. 그는 자신이 동인도에 있다고 생각했다. 그 이유로 아메리카 원주민들이 '인디언'이라고 불렀다.

사실 이곳이 '신세계'라는 것을 깨달은 사람은 바로 또 다른 항해사인 아메리고 베스푸치였다. 그것이 아메리카 대륙을 그의 이름을 따서 부르게 된 이유이다. 그러나, 콜럼버스는 유럽인들의 관심을 아메리카로 가져온 사람이었다. 아마도 그것이 그가 아메리카를 발견했다고 많은 사람들이 믿는 이유일 것이다.

어휘
discover[diskʌ́vər] 동 발견하다 (discovery 명 발견)   fact[fækt] 명 사실   ancestor[ǽnsestər] 명 조상, 선조   European[jùərəpíən] 명 유럽인   reach[ríːʃ] 동 …에 이르다, 도달하다 evidence[évədəns] 명 증거, 흔적   northern[nɔ́ːrðərn] 형 북부의   nearly[níərli] 부 거의 eastern[íːstərn] 형 동쪽의   navigator[nǽvəgèitər] 명 항해사   realize[ríːəlàiz] 동 깨닫다 continent[kántənənt] 명 대륙   name after …의 이름을 따서 명명하다   attention[əténʃən] 명 관심, 주목   [문제] explorer[iksplɔ́ːrər] 명 탐험가   unfamiliar[ʌ̀nfəmíljər] 형 익숙지 않은 prove[pruːv] 동 증명하다   exist[igzíst] 동 존재하다   lie[lai] 동 거짓말하다 achievement[ətʃíːvmənt] 명 업적

구문
8행 First, there were people [**who** found America earlier than Columbus].
  • who 이하는 people을 수식하는 주격 관계대명사절
11행 They **had** already **been living** there since their ancestors moved across ….
  • had been living: '…해 오고 있었다'라는 의미의 과거완료 진행
13행 Scientists found evidence [**that** the Vikings *had been* in the northern part of America].
  • that: evidence와 동격인 명사절을 이끄는 접속사
  • had been: 과거 기준 시점까지 계속된 상태나 동작을 나타내는 과거완료
16행 Moreover, when Columbus arrived in America, he didn't even know [**where** he was].
  • where 이하는 '의문사 + 주어 + 동사' 어순의 간접의문문으로, 동사 know의 목적어 역할을 함

STRATEGIC SUMMARY   discovered, European, India, wrong

VOCABULARY REVIEW

A *1* believe *2* scientist *3* ancestor *4* agree
B *1* c *2* d   C *1* c *2* b *3* c *4* b

unit
19 ENVIRONMENT   pp. 81-84

VOCABULARY PREVIEW

A *1* d *2* a *3* c *4* b   B *1* throw away *2* collect *3* separate *4* brand-new

⋆*Urban Mining*

1 d   **2** c, d   **3** its sources are materials in the city   **4** c   **5** c

> 매해, 오래된 휴대전화와 컴퓨터를 포함해 수천 톤의 전자 폐기물이 버려진다. 이것은 자원을 낭비할 뿐만 아니라 환경에 해를 끼친다. 다행히, 도시 광산업이 이 문제를 해결할 수 있다.
>
> 도시 광산업은 새롭게 발달된 산업이다. 그것은 오래된 전자기기에서 구리, 은, 그리고 심지어 금과 같은 금속을 얻는 것을 수반한다. 그것의 원천이 도시에 있는 재료들이라서, 그것은 '도시' 광산업이라고 불린다. 그 일은 어떻게 돌아가는가? 우선, 오래된 전자기기들이 수집되어 작은 부분으로 쪼개진다. 그러고 나서, 그것들은 가치 있는 금속을 분리하기 위해 처리된다. 언젠가, 이 금속들은 신제품으로 다시 태어날 것이다!
>
> 도시 광산업은 두 가지 이유로 인기를 얻고 있다. 첫째로, 그것은 실제 광산업보다 더 경제적이다. 사실, 1톤의 바위보다 1톤의 휴대전화에 30배 더 많은 금이 있다. 그것은 또한 환경에 도움이 된다. 도시 광산업을 통해서, 우리는 오래된 전자 제품을 재활용할 수 있고, 귀중한 천연자원을 재사용할 수 있다. 우리가 도시 광산업을 더 개발하면 할수록, 우리의 환경은 더 건강해질 것이다!

어휘 electronic[ilektránik] 형 전자의 (electronics 명 (*pl.*) 전자기기)   waste[weist] 명 폐기물 동 낭비하다   throw away 버리다   resource[rí:sɔːrs] 명 자원   harm[haːrm] 동 해를 끼치다   urban[ə́:rbən] 형 도시의   solve[salv] 동 해결하다   industry[índəstri] 명 산업   metal[métl] 명 금속   copper[kápər] 명 구리   source[sɔːrs] 명 원천, 근원   material[mətíəriəl] 명 재료   collect[kəlékt] 동 모으다, 수집하다   process[práses] 동 처리하다   separate[sépərèit] 동 분리하다, 나누다   valuable[væljuəbl] 형 소중한, 가치가 큰   brand-new[brǽndnjúː] 형 아주 새로운   economical[èkənámikəl] 형 경제적인   recycle[riːsáikl] 동 재활용하다   reuse[riːjúːz] 동 재사용하다   precious[préʃəs] 형 귀중한   [문제] benefit[bénəfit] 명 이득   have an effect on …에 영향을 미치다   replace[ripléis] 동 대체하다, 대신하다

구문 2행   This **not only** wastes resources **but also** harms the environment.
  • not only A but also B: A뿐만 아니라 B도
  5행   **As** its sources are materials in the city, it's called "urban" mining.
  • as: 이유를 나타내는 접속사
  11행   In fact, there's **30 times more** gold in a ton of cellphones **than** in a ton of rock.
  • 배수사 + 비교급 + than: …보다 ~배 더 …한
  15행   **The more** we develop urban mining, **the healthier** our environment will become!
  • the + 비교급 …, the + 비교급 ~: …하면 할수록 더 ~하다

STRATEGIC ORGANIZER   electronic, gathered, economical, healthier

VOCABULARY REVIEW

A **1** valuable   **2** industry   **3** resource   **4** recycle
B **1** c **2** b   **C** **1** b **2** a **3** b **4** d

CULTURE

pp. 85-88

VOCABULARY PREVIEW

A **1** c **2** a **3** d **4** b   **B** **1** beginning   **2** welcome   **3** rich   **4** prefer

★Foods for the New Year

1 c **2** c **3** b **4** they think their life might go in the wrong direction if they eat lobster **5** a

---

연초에는 전 세계 사람들이 서로 다른 방식으로 새해를 맞이한다. 그것들 중 한 가지는 <u>당신에게 행운을 가져다줄</u> 특별한 음식을 먹는 것이다.

그렇다면 사람들은 어떤 음식을 먹을까? 스페인에서는 사람들이 새해 전날 자정에 열두 알의 포도를 먹는다. 사람들은 열두 알의 포도를 먹는 것이 그들에게 열두 달 동안 행복을 가져다줄 것이라 생각한다. 서유럽에서는 사람들이 양배추 같은 녹색 채소를 선호한다. (녹색 채소는 당신의 눈에 좋다.) 이 채소들은 접힌 지폐처럼 생겼다. 그래서 사람들은 그것들을 먹음으로써 자신이 부유해질 수 있다고 믿는다. 중국과 일본 같은 몇몇 아시아 국가에서는 사람들이 긴 국수를 먹는다. 그들은 긴 국수가 장수를 상징한다고 생각한다.

하지만 새해 무렵 사람들이 피하는 몇 음식들도 있다. 예를 들어, 몇몇 사람들은 바닷가재를 먹으면 자신의 삶이 잘못된 방향으로 갈지도 모른다고 생각한다. 이는 바닷가재가 뒤로 움직이기 때문이다.

새해에 어떤 행운의 요리를 즐기든 너무 많이 먹지는 마라. 그렇지 않으면 다이어트를 하면서 새해를 시작해야 할 테니까 말이다!

어휘 beginning[biɡíniŋ] 명 초, 시작   welcome[wélkəm] 동 맞이하다, 환영하다   midnight[mídnàit] 명 자정   happiness[hǽpinis] 명 행복   prefer[prifə́ːr] 동 선호하다   cabbage[kǽbidʒ] 명 양배추   fold[fould] 동 접다   rich[ritʃ] 형 부유한   noodle[núːdl] 명 (pl.) 국수   symbolize[símbəlàiz] 동 상징하다   avoid[əvɔ́id] 동 피하다   direction[dirékʃən] 명 방향   lobster[lάbstər] 명 바닷가재   backward[bǽkwərd] 부 뒤쪽으로   dish[diʃ] 명 요리   [문제] resolution[rèzəlúːʃən] 명 결심   fortune[fɔ́ːrtʃən] 명 운, 행운   stand for …을 나타내다[의미하다]

구문 3행 One of them is to eat a special food [**that** will bring you good fortune].
- that 이하는 a special food를 수식하는 주격 관계대명사절

7행 People think (that) [**eating** 12 grapes] will bring them happiness for 12 months.
- eating 이하는 that절의 주어로 쓰인 동명사구

19행 **Whichever** lucky dish you enjoy for the New Year, don't eat it too much.
- whichever: '어느 …이든지'라는 의미의 복합관계형용사

STRATEGIC SUMMARY New Year, happiness, money, avoid

VOCABULARY REVIEW

A **1** backward **2** eve **3** fold **4** direction
B **1** b **2** c   C **1** d **2** a **3** b **4** c

MEMO

MEMO